Teens and MENTAL HEALTH

By Elisabeth Herschbach

San Diego, CA

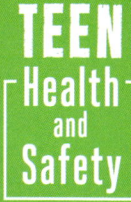

TEEN Health and Safety

© 2019 ReferencePoint Press, Inc.
Printed in the United States

For more information, contact:
ReferencePoint Press, Inc.
PO Box 27779
San Diego, CA 92198
www.ReferencePointPress.com

ALL RIGHTS RESERVED.

No part of this work covered by the copyright hereon may be reproduced or used in any form or by any means—graphic, electronic, or mechanical, including photocopying, recording, taping, web distribution, or information storage retrieval systems—without the written permission of the publisher.

Content Consultant: Donna L. Londino, MD, Professor, Department of Psychiatry and Health Behavior, Medical College of Georgia, Augusta University

LIBRARY OF CONGRESS CATALOGING-IN-PUBLICATION DATA

Name: Herschbach, Elisabeth, author.
Title: Teen Mental Health / by Elisabeth Herschbach.
Description: San Diego, CA : ReferencePoint Press, Inc., [2019] | Series:
   Teen Health and Safety | Audience: Grade 9 to 12. |
   Includes bibliographical references and index.
Identifiers: LCCN 2018011551 (print) | LCCN 2018012118 (ebook) | ISBN
   9781682825105 (ebook) | ISBN 9781682825099 (hardback)
Subjects: LCSH: Adolescent psychopathology—Juvenile literature. | Teenagers—Mental health—
   Juvenile literature. | Emotions—Juvenile literature. | Thought and thinking—Juvenile literature.
Classification: LCC RJ503 (ebook) | LCC RJ503 .H37 2019 (print) | DDC   616.8900835—dc23
LC record available at https://lccn.loc.gov/2018011551

CONTENTS

Introduction   4
   ERASING THE STIGMA OF MENTAL ILLNESS

Chapter 1   8
   WHAT IS MENTAL HEALTH?

Chapter 2   22
   WHAT CAUSES MENTAL HEALTH PROBLEMS?

Chapter 3   36
   WHAT ARE THE EFFECTS OF MENTAL HEALTH PROBLEMS?

Chapter 4   50
   HOW CAN TEENS GET HELP?

Recognizing Signs of Trouble/Organizations to Contact   68
Source Notes   70
For Further Research   74
Index   76
Image Credits   79
About the Author   80

Introduction

ERASING THE STIGMA OF MENTAL ILLNESS

Cait Irwin had a happy and ordinary childhood. She was a friendly and outgoing child. She had loving parents, an older brother, and two dogs. She loved art, played softball, and enjoyed hanging out with friends. But in the middle of eighth grade, Cait found herself bursting into tears at the slightest setback. She felt overwhelmed by constant anxiety. She dreaded getting out of bed in the morning.

At first, her parents and teachers thought Cait was experiencing the moodiness of adolescence. Puberty is a time of drastic physical and emotional changes, as well as difficult transitions between childhood and adulthood. The teen years can be stressful and confusing. It's normal to feel anxious and melancholy at times.

But what Cait was experiencing went far beyond moodiness. She felt exhausted all the time but had trouble sleeping at night. Her appetite waned and she lost weight. She had trouble concentrating. Her grades started slipping. She found it hard to accomplish even the simplest of tasks. She felt crushed by feelings of hopelessness. She even found herself considering suicide. "I was sliding downhill fast, and I didn't know what had pushed me over the edge or how to stop the descent," she wrote in her memoir *Monochrome Days*. "The darkness was spreading inside me like a cancer."[1]

After months of suffering, Cait finally sought help. She was diagnosed with major depression, sometimes also called clinical depression. The National Institute of Mental Health defines depression as a mood disorder that "causes severe symptoms that affect how you feel, think, and handle daily activities, such as sleeping, eating, or working."[2] In Cait's words, "It drains your hope, saps your energy, and steals all the fun from your life."[3]

> "[Depression] drains your hope, saps your energy, and steals all the fun from your life."[3]
>
> —Cait Irwin, author, artist, and mental health advocate

With the help of medication and therapy, Cait was able to recover and regain control of her life. Today, she lives a full and successful life as an artist, writer, and mental health advocate. "Depression can feel unchangeable, but that's a nasty trick the disease plays on your mind," she says. "In truth, it is something you *can* change with effort, patience, and the help of appropriate treatment."[4]

Mental Health Problems Are Medical Problems

Millions of Americans of all ages suffer from depression or other mental health conditions. According to some estimates, mental illness is more common than diabetes, heart disease, or cancer. Among teens and school-aged children specifically, mental health problems are more common than any other type of health issue.

Yet there are still many misperceptions and negative stereotypes about mental illness. All too often, being labeled with a mental health disorder comes with a stigma, or a sense of social disapproval and shame. As a result, many people who struggle with their mental health are afraid to seek out the treatment they need. As former US Surgeon

General David Satcher reported in 1999, "Nearly half of all Americans who have a severe mental illness do not seek treatment."[5] In many cases, reluctance to seek treatment is caused by the stigma attached to mental illness.

Mental health issues are medical problems, not personal failings or character flaws. Struggling with depression, anxiety, or other mental health challenges is not any more shameful than having asthma, diabetes, or arthritis. And just like other medical problems, mental health problems can be treated.

An Early Start

Left untreated, mental illness can severely impact a person's quality of life and emotional well-being. It can make it harder to succeed in school and in the workplace. It can also take a toll on personal relationships. The stakes are even higher for teens and young people. Three-quarters of all mental health problems start before the age of twenty-four. That's why it's imperative for teens and young adults to understand the signs and symptoms of mental health disorders.

The symptoms of a mental illness can be controlled with the right treatment. Most people diagnosed with mental disorders can live fully functioning, productive lives. In fact, many highly successful public figures have tackled mental illness at some point in their lives.

Reflecting on her own battle with depression, Irwin notes, "With medication and psychotherapy—plus a healthy dose of self-help—I ultimately

> **"[N]early half of all Americans who have a severe mental illness do not seek treatment."[5]**
>
> —former US Surgeon General David Satcher

(clockwise from top left) Ted Turner, Lady Gaga, Gabourey Sidibe, Michael Phelps, and J. K. Rowling have struggled with mental illness at one time or another. All have been open about their history with mental illness to minimize its stigma.

managed to take back my life and rediscover my reasons for living it."[6] That's the case for the millions of other teens and adults who travel a similar road to recovery with their own mental health disorders.

Chapter 1

WHAT IS MENTAL HEALTH?

The American Psychological Association defines mental health as "the way your thoughts, feelings, and behaviors affect your life."[7] Being in good mental health gives us a sense of emotional, psychological, and social well-being. It helps us make sound decisions, set and fulfill meaningful personal goals, and develop healthy social relationships. It gives us the resilience to handle stress, cope with setbacks and challenges, and adapt to changes. It supports our continued emotional and psychological growth. According to the World Health Organization, mental health is "fundamental to our collective and individual ability as humans to think, emote, interact with each other, earn a living and enjoy life."[8]

Mental health problems cause persistent symptoms that negatively affect how one thinks, feels, acts, or relates to others. These symptoms cause emotional pain, anxiety, and disordered thinking. They may interfere with schooling, work, and social relationships. They may even make it hard to keep up with the basic tasks of everyday life.

A Matter of Degree

It can sometimes be hard to tell if specific feelings and behaviors are a sign of a mental health problem or if they fall within the range

Mood swings and periods of sadness are a normal part of being a teenager. Cause for concern arises when one's moods and feelings negatively affect one's ability to lead a full and healthy life.

of normal human experience. Everyone experiences sadness, stress, anxiety, and negative thoughts from time to time, and many people find it hard to cope when they hit a rough patch. For teens in particular, varying emotions and moods are a normal part of development. So is a certain amount of gloominess and angst. The difference between ordinary emotional struggles and mental health problems comes down to degree and duration. As the US Department of Health and Human Services defines them, mental illnesses are conditions "characterized by alterations in thinking, mood, or behavior (or some combination thereof) associated with distress and/or impaired functioning."[9] In other words, negative mental and emotional states become a problem when they have a serious impact on a person's life. Psychological symptoms that are very intense, last a long time or occur very frequently, and significantly disrupt daily life may be signs of an illness.

MENTAL HEALTH AND CULTURAL NORMS

Mental illness is often stigmatized because it can't easily be seen or quantified. Physical diseases, such as diabetes and cancer, manifest themselves as bodily changes or physical impairments that stand out as unusual. They can be tested and measured. Mental illnesses, by contrast, involve behaviors, feelings, and thoughts. Those can't be tested or measured. There isn't always a clear dividing line marking the difference between healthy and unhealthy behaviors, feelings, and thoughts. Instead, it depends on what is seen as normal or abnormal for the context.

However, conceptions of normality are shaped by societal expectations. This means mental health is, at least in part, a culturally bound concept. In other words, judgments about which behaviors, feelings, and thoughts are normal can differ across cultures and times. For example, in the 1960s the American Psychiatric Association classified homosexuality as a mental dysfunction. Today it is commonly accepted in the United States that differences in sexual preferences simply reflect the range of normal human variations that occur in nature.

The fact that cultural attitudes and beliefs can influence how we understand mental illness makes the concept of mental health harder to pin down. It also means mental health professionals need to take cultural context into consideration when working with patients from different cultural backgrounds.

For example, it is normal to feel stressed out about a big test, an important job interview, or a difficult personal situation. It isn't normal to have constant bouts of crippling anxiety over little things like getting on the bus every morning or taking a precise number of steps down the stairs. According to mental health experts, such excessive levels of anxiety may be pathological, or a sign of a disorder. As Terje Ogden and Kristine Amlund Hagen write in their book *Adolescent Mental Health*, "It is when anxious feelings interfere with daily activities and ultimately impede normal developmental tasks that the anxious feelings and emotions can be considered pathological."[10]

Many teens experience emotional ups and downs. Very intense and persistent mood swings, however, may indicate a mood disorder. As clinical psychologist Linda Wilmshurst says, "For individuals suffering from mood disorders, depressed or elated states can be extreme and long lasting, causing problems with day-to-day functioning."[11]

The Many Faces of Mental Illness

Although the term *mental illness* is often used in the singular, mental illness is not a single condition with a uniform set of features. Symptoms vary from person to person, and mental illnesses come in many types and degrees. Different disorders affect one's behavior, emotions, thought patterns, and personality in different ways.

For example, eating disorders such as bulimia and anorexia nervosa cause severe distress about body weight and food intake. Obsessive-compulsive disorder (OCD) involves recurring unwanted thoughts and actions that feel out of a person's control. A person with OCD may compulsively engage in fixed rituals, such as excessive hand washing. Schizophrenia causes psychosis, or a state of being out of touch with reality. People with this disorder experience episodes of severely disorganized and confused thought and speech. These episodes often consist of hallucinations, or sensations of things that are not real, and delusions, which are fixed ideas that do not correspond with reality.

These are just a few of the many types of mental disorders that teens can experience. The fifth edition of the *Diagnostic and Statistical Manual of Mental Disorders* (*DSM*), published by the American Psychiatric Association, lists 541 different diagnostic categories.

The most common types of mental illnesses experienced by teens include anxiety disorders, which cause excessive feelings of fear, uneasiness, worry, and stress, and depressive disorders, which cause persistent feelings of sadness and low mood.

Anxiety Disorders

Stress and fear serve an important biological function as key components in the body's defense mechanism against possible threats in the environment. Feelings of stress and fear trigger what scientists call the "fight or flight response." This is a chain of physical and mental responses that help us avoid danger and respond appropriately to potential threats. "This primitive, hard-wired emotional response prepares us for the strenuous motor efforts required for fighting or running," says Harvard Medical School psychiatrist John Ratey. "A fearful stimulus primes the body with adrenaline and prompts the fastest physical reaction possible."[12]

From an evolutionary point of view, this mechanism is essential to ensuring human survival. Stress also plays an important function in everyday life. For example, stress can motivate people to work harder and study longer. It keeps one on one's toes, giving the extra push needed to exert more effort and perform at optimum levels.

> **"A fearful stimulus primes the body with adrenaline and prompts the fastest physical reaction possible."[12]**
>
> —Dr. John Ratey, Harvard Medical School psychiatrist

In people with anxiety disorders, however, feelings of stress and fear are so excessive they cause distress and dysfunction. The emotional responses that normally protect people from harm instead become harmful themselves.

Anxiety disorders take on different forms. Some people feel intense fear and anxiety in reaction to specific triggers. For example, people with social anxiety disorder have a severe and persistent fear of being judged or rejected by others in social situations. People with phobias experience episodes of extreme fear in response to certain objects or situations, such as spiders, heights, or being in crowded places. Other people suffer from a generalized state of excessive, persistent anxiety that isn't focused on any single object, situation, or event. This is known as generalized anxiety disorder (GAD).

People with GAD are almost constantly in a state of extreme anxiety and fear that is disproportionate to any actual threat or risk. In addition to crippling levels of anxiety, people suffering from GAD also experience other psychological symptoms, such as fatigue, trouble concentrating, and irritability. These psychological symptoms are typically accompanied by bodily reactions such as headaches and stomach aches or intestinal problems.

Many people with anxiety suffer from more than one distinct anxiety disorder at the same time. For example, in her memoir *On the Edge: A Journey through Anxiety*, journalist Andrea Petersen describes how the symptoms of four different anxiety disorders interfered with her daily life:

> *I was having panic attacks—sudden, intense periods of blinding terror, rapid breathing, and chest pain—several times of the day (diagnosis: panic disorder). The rest of the time, I was worried, living with the nervous expectation of imminent disaster (diagnosis: generalized anxiety disorder, or GAD). I had developed a long list of particular fears, too: dentists, flying, driving on highways, taking medication, touching dirt, using a new tube of toothpaste, and licking envelopes. I did my best to avoid them all (diagnosis: specific phobia). My world was becoming smaller and smaller as more places became*

Anxiety disorders stem from an excessive, persistent feeling of fear beyond humans' natural instinct for safety. Some anxiety disorders are triggered by a certain stimulus while others are more general.

> no-go zones: movie theaters, stadiums, lines. The potential for panic attacks—and the difficulty of escape—was too great (diagnosis: agoraphobia).[13]

Trauma and Mental Health

Acute fear and stress triggered by traumatic experiences belong to a separate category known as Trauma and Stressor-Related Disorders. The best known of these is post-traumatic stress disorder (PTSD). Many of the symptoms of PTSD are similar to those of anxiety disorders, so much so that PTSD was once classified as an anxiety disorder itself. The *DSM*'s development of a PTSD category emphasizes PTSD's defining feature: a link between one's symptoms and a traumatic event.

PTSD occurs in response to traumatic events involving "actual or threatened death, serious injury, or sexual violence," according to the *DSM*'s definition.[14] Examples might include natural disasters, violent crimes, sexual abuse, war, or terrorist attacks. Researchers have found that compared to survivors of other types of traumas, survivors of rape and assault are at an especially high risk of PTSD.

Symptoms of PTSD include intense fear and anxiety, feelings of guilt and self-blame, agitated behavior, social withdrawal, and feelings of emotional numbness. People with the disorder often show an inability to remember key details of the traumatic event yet persistently avoid places, people, or situations associated with the triggering event. They may repeatedly relive the trauma through recurring flashbacks, nightmares, and intrusive thoughts and images.

In teens, PTSD is associated with impulsive, self-destructive behaviors. "Adolescents tend to reenact trauma through risk-taking behavior that can increase the chances of more stressful consequences," Wilmshurst notes.[15] For example, teens suffering from PTSD may express their trauma by engaging in high-risk behaviors, such as unsafe sexual practices, driving recklessly, abusing drugs or alcohol, running away, or getting in trouble at school or with the law. "The impact of severe trauma at adolescence can be particularly devastating and life altering," Wilmshurst says.[16]

Depressive Disorders

Like trauma, depression can have particularly damaging effects on teens. Researchers have found that teens who have suffered from depression are at greater risk of experiencing personal and social problems as adults. This includes future mental health issues, problems with employment and interpersonal relationships, and drug and alcohol use.

Depression is a mood disorder. As the name suggests, mood disorders disrupt one's ability to regulate moods, which are the emotional states that color one's experiences of the world and give them an emotional charge. As with all mental health problems, mood disorders come in different degrees and varieties.

Major depressive disorder (MDD) causes disabling episodes of negative emotional states, including extreme sadness, loss of interest in daily activities, and feelings of emptiness, helplessness, hopelessness, and worthlessness. Without treatment, people with MDD experience an average of five to seven episodes of major depression over their life. Typically, the episodes get increasingly worse over time. Depressed states in people with MDD last for at least two weeks at a time and are typically accompanied by negative behavioral patterns such as withdrawal from social situations, fatigue, changes in energy level, and disruptions of eating and sleeping patterns. Some teens exhibit their depression by being excessively grouchy, aggressive, or negative, or by acting out and getting in trouble at school.

> **"Adolescents tend to reenact trauma through risk-taking behavior that can increase the chances of more stressful consequences."[15]**
>
> —Linda Wilmshurst, clinical psychologist

Persistent depressive disorder (PDD) is a chronic, or long-lasting, form of depression. Its symptoms are similar to those of MDD but less severe and experienced on a long-term basis. Although the

TERMS OF THE TRADE

Many of the terms used to talk about health conditions sound similar. Keeping them straight can be confusing. For example, what is the difference between a disease and a disorder? What about a sign and a symptom? These pairs of terms are often used interchangeably, but there are some differences in meaning.

A disease is an abnormal state of health with a known cause and clearly defined, specific characteristics. It is caused by structural change in some part or parts of the body. It impairs normal functioning. And it is characterized by concrete signs and symptoms. The term *disorder* is used more generally to refer to any condition that disrupts normal functioning in some way. The term does not imply, however, that the cause is known or that there are any identified structural changes in the body.

Signs of an illness are features that a doctor, nurse, or other external person detects in a patient. They are objective in the sense that they are observable and measurable indicators of a problem. Symptoms are the features or states that a person experiences, such as feelings of fatigue, confusion, or sadness. These are the complaints that a patient reports to a doctor or practitioner. They are subjective in the sense that they can't be directly felt by an outside person. Finally, when certain signs and symptoms routinely occur, the combined pattern is referred to as a syndrome.

negative emotional states associated with PDD are less intense, they still make it difficult for people with this condition to feel good and function normally.

Bipolar disorder involves wild fluctuations between states of depression and states of mania, which are periods of extreme euphoria, or excessive enthusiasm, excitement, and happiness. During manic states, people with bipolar disorder feel intense mental highs. These are accompanied by an inflated sense of self-esteem,

People affected by bipolar disorder often liken it to an emotional roller coaster. Extreme highs are usually followed by extreme lows.

heightened energy levels, less need for sleep, and increased involvement in risky behaviors.

"The playful, mind-expanding sense of euphoria that mania can bring can last for moments, days, or weeks," Patrick Jamieson explains in *Mind Race: A Firsthand Account of One Teenager's Experience with Bipolar Disorder*.[17] But eventually the mental rush leads to a crash. "It's great for a time, but it doesn't last," Jamieson writes. "What follows isn't worth the exhilaration of the earlier euphoria. My mania is a mountain from which I abruptly plunge into depression."[18]

Evolutionary Blues

As with anxiety and stress, the moods and emotions associated with depression are rooted in biological functions with an evolutionary purpose. Psychological pain prompts one to withdraw from harmful situations. When linked to loss, sadness motivates one to seek out the lost object, which is a crucial response in the bond between children and their attachment figures.

Intriguingly, researchers have also uncovered links between depression and the body's responses to infection. Genetic variations associated with depression appear to improve the functioning of the immune system. Some depressive symptoms may have even helped previous generations limit the effects of disease. Social withdrawal, for example, limits one's exposure to further infections. Low energy prompts the body to minimize activities and thus preserve all of its energy for fighting infection. University of Arizona psychiatrist Charles Raison explains, "The basic idea is that depression and the genes that promote it were very adaptive for helping people—especially young children—not die of infection in the ancestral environment."[19]

But for teens and adults in the modern world, the symptoms of depression can turn toxic. The World Health Organization ranks MDD as the fourth leading cause of disability worldwide. Depression can derail a person's ability to work, study, succeed in school, maintain friendships, and enjoy life. In teens, it can hinder emotional growth and development. As the leading risk factor for suicide in the United States, it can also be deadly.

Suicide and Self-Harm

Suicide is the second leading cause of death among teens. Only accidents claim more teen lives. According to the Centers for Disease Control and Prevention (CDC), more than 2,000 American teens between the ages of fifteen and nineteen committed suicide in 2015. For every teen who dies by suicide, another one hundred to two hundred attempt it. According to the Jason Foundation, a suicide prevention organization, an average of 3,470 high-school-aged teens attempt suicide every day in the United States. In 2015, 18 percent of American high school students reported thinking seriously about suicide during the preceding year.

In the majority of cases, mental health disorders are behind suicidal thoughts and behavior. More than 90 percent of people who die by suicide in the United States have a diagnosable mental health illness at the time of their death. As many as two-thirds have some form of depressive disorder. According to psychologists Gerald Koocher and Annette La Greca, "The single best way to prevent suicide involves early recognition and treatment of mental illnesses."[20]

> "The single best way to prevent suicide involves early recognition and treatment of mental illnesses."[20]
>
> —Gerald Koocher and Annette La Greca, psychologists

Depression, anxiety, and other mental health problems are also risk factors for what mental health experts call non-suicidal self-injury (NSSI). NSSI, or self-harm, refers to deliberate acts of self-injury, such as cutting or burning of the skin, that are not meant to be suicide attempts. As many as one-third of all teens engage in self-harming behaviors. Experts say a majority of self-harming teens meet the diagnostic criteria for at least one mental health disorder. Two-thirds meet the criteria for depression specifically.

Although acts of self-harm aren't indicative of suicidal intent, they do raise the risk of future suicide attempts. Experts agree self-harm serves as a type of "suicide training" for some teens. But in most

Teens afflicted with mental health disorders are at greater risk for alcohol and drug abuse, as well as self-harm and suicide.

cases, self-harm is a strategy for coping with acute psychological distress, including deep sadness, anxiety, or feelings of numbness. Victoria Leatham, for example, poignantly describes how she began cutting herself in her twenties as a means of coping with anxiety, depression, and an eating disorder. "Relief was what I was looking for," she writes in her memoir *Bloodletting: A True Story of Secrets, Self-Harm and Survival*. "What I wanted—what I needed—was a pain I could see and deal with. I couldn't cope with the mess inside me any longer. . . . I wanted real, tangible, physical pain. That I could understand."[21]

Chapter 2

WHAT CAUSES MENTAL HEALTH PROBLEMS?

Historically, mental illness has been blamed on a wide range of causes, from supernatural forces to bad parenting. In much of the ancient and medieval world, mental illness was seen as the work of evil spirits or demons. Up into the eighteenth century in Europe, the preferred theory was that mental health problems were caused by an imbalance of "humors"—four fluids thought to be basic elements of the body. And in the mid-twentieth century, many American psychiatrists believed dysfunctional mothers were to blame for making their children ill with mental health disorders such as schizophrenia.

Today, it is widely recognized that all mental health problems are rooted in disorders of the brain. Nobel Prize–winning neuroscientist Eric Kandel says, "All mental processes, even the most complex psychological processes, derive from operations of the brain."[22] When these operations malfunction, mental health problems arise.

It's All in Your Head

The human brain is the most complex structure in the known universe. It is a vast network of approximately 86 billion specialized cells called neurons. Neurons communicate with other neurons in the brain, using more than one hundred different chemical substances called

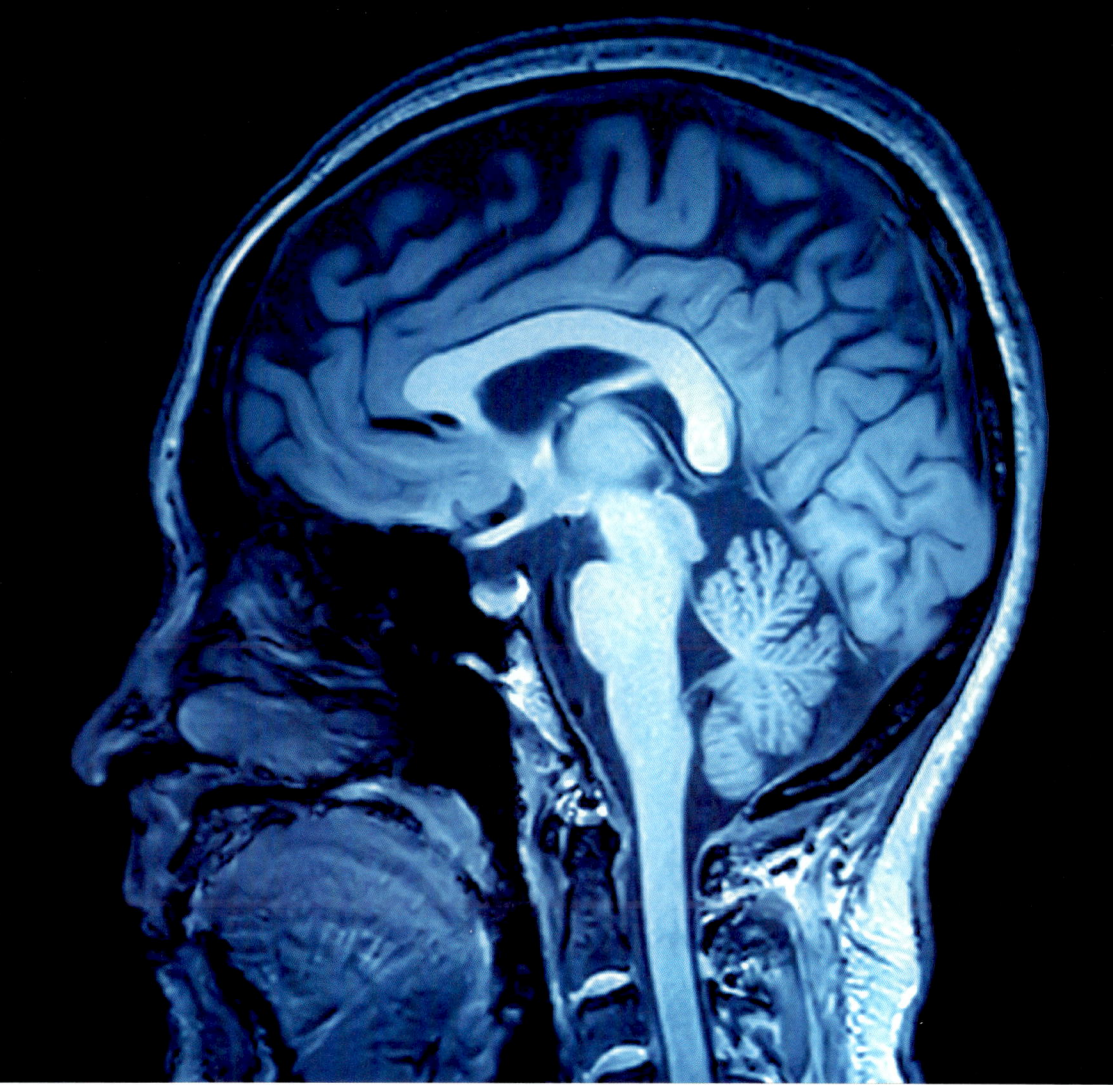

The human brain, shown here in an MRI image, is the source of all mental health disorders. These disorders are caused by defects in the brain's circuitry.

neurotransmitters. These chemical messengers transmit signals from cell to cell, shuttling information back and forth that tells the cells how to respond.

At any moment, a single neuron may be communicating with tens of thousands of other neurons, creating a web of trillions of constantly changing connections across different regions of the brain. In total, the number of different patterns of connections that are possible in a single brain is an eye-popping 40 quadrillion.

The brain's neurons are organized into dozens of structures that perform specialized functions. Each structure communicates with other brain structures, forming circuits, or information loops, made up of patterned connections. University of California, San Diego neuroscientist V. S. Ramachandran explains, "Circuits pass information back and forth in repeating loops, and allow brain structures to work together to create sophisticated perceptions, thoughts, and behaviors."[23] Everything we do, feel, think, perceive, and remember relies on the brain's ability to coordinate these delicately balanced processes. Given how complex they are, it is no surprise that there are sometimes glitches.

The Brain Science of Mental Illness

Scientists use various brain imagining techniques to gain insight into what happens in the brain when things go wrong. Such techniques allow doctors and researchers to measure brain activity or look for defects in specific brain structures. For example, computed tomography (CT) scans create a picture of structures in the brain using X-ray equipment. Functional magnetic resonance imaging (fMRI) allows scientists to track changes in blood flow to different regions of the brain. Because blood flow to a specific area increases when that region of the brain is in use, this technique helps scientists see how specific areas respond or fail to respond to particular tasks or stimuli.

Based on brain research using these imaging techniques, scientists think that many mental disorders are linked to abnormalities in the functioning of certain brain circuits. For example, researchers at Stanford University School of Medicine found that negative stimuli seem to be processed differently in the brains of patients with anxiety. These differences may explain why people with anxiety disorders may have problems regulating their emotional responses to stress.

GOT GABA?

Brain research can help scientists better understand malfunctions in the brain that may increase a person's risk of mental illness. But sometimes it can also help to identify the protective mechanisms that keep brains healthy. For example, researchers from the University of Cambridge in the United Kingdom have found that a neurotransmitter known as GABA, active in the hippocampus, plays a role helping people to suppress intrusive, unwanted thoughts. Recurring, unwanted thoughts are a symptom of several mental health disorders, including anxiety, PTSD, depression, and schizophrenia.

Understanding how healthy people are able to inhibit such thoughts could be a step forward in developing treatments for those with disorders. "What's exciting about this is that now we're getting very specific," says Michael Anderson, a member of the research team. "Before, we could only say 'this part of the brain acts on that part,' but now we can say which neurotransmitters are likely important—and as a result, infer the role of inhibitory neurons—in enabling us to stop unwanted thoughts."

Quoted in Ben Coxworth, "Plagued by Unwanted Thoughts? You May Be Low on Hippocampal GABA," *New Atlas*, November 6, 2017. newatlas.com.

According to another study, people with anxiety may even have trouble perceiving the difference between stressful experiences and those that are neutral. "Our study suggests that people with anxiety cannot discriminate, at the most basic level, between stimuli that have an emotional content and similar mundane or daily stimuli," says Rony Paz of the Weizmann Institute of Science in Rehovot, Israel. "This in turn might explain the anxious response that they exhibit to scenarios that seem regular, normal or non-emotional to anyone else—their brain cannot discriminate and responds as if it is the anxious stimulus."[24]

Some studies have linked mental health problems with changes in specific structures in the brain. For example, the amygdala, a part of the brain where emotional memories are stored, appears to be enlarged in many patients with mood and anxiety disorders. This is thought to cause abnormal levels of stress hormones and other chemicals that affect mood and cognition.

And in some cases, scientists have been able to identify specific neurotransmitters that interfere with normal patterns of neural connections. For example, studies have shown that some people with depression have fewer receptors for serotonin, a neurotransmitter, in their hippocampus. The hippocampus is an area of the brain that acts as a gateway between memory and mood. This may disrupt the communication loop in brain circuits involved in regulating moods and many cognitive functions, such as learning and memory. "The hippocampus often is the key to interpreting things such as whether an experience is good or bad, whether a person is looking at me with a happy face or a sad face, whether that person is angry with me, those sorts of things," radiologist and psychiatrist Mark A. Mintun says.[25] The relationship between the hippocampus and its serotonin neurotransmitters sheds light on how the brain works in people with depression.

> "People with anxiety cannot discriminate . . . between stimuli that have an emotional content and similar mundane or daily stimuli."[24]
>
> —Rony Paz, the Weizmann Institute of Science

Complex Interactions

Thanks to brain scanning techniques, scientists are developing a better understanding of the relationships between different parts and functions of the brain. Eventually this may help them locate specific areas and neural processes of the brain that are linked to mental illnesses. However, people are a long way from being able to pin down the specific causes behind disorders of the brain. Most researchers think there is no single variable that explains why some people develop mental illnesses. Instead, these conditions arise from complex interactions between genetic, biological, psychological, social, and environmental factors.

Research shows that having a close family member with a mental illness significantly raises the risk of developing mental health problems. For example, children of depressed parents are three times more likely to develop depression, anxiety, or substance abuse problems than their peers without depressed parents. A similar pattern holds for many other mental disorders, including schizophrenia. When one parent has schizophrenia, children have an estimated 10 percent chance of developing the illness themselves. This is compared to an only 1 percent risk in the general population. When both parents are schizophrenic, the odds jump to approximately 40 percent.

But how much of this increased risk is due to factors in the family environment, such as an unstable upbringing or emotional stress in the household? How much is genetic, or determined by inherited genes? Genes are segments of DNA, the basic hereditary material found in almost every cell in the body. Passed on from parents to children, genes contain instructions for how our bodies develop and function. Scientists know they play an important role in shaping the way our brains develop. That includes the development of mental disorders. But specifying the exact role genes play is more challenging.

A Family Affair

To estimate the effect of genes on mental health, scientists study twins raised in different households. If adopted twins and those raised by their biological parents have similar rates of developing certain mental illnesses, then this may be an important clue about the effect of genes over environment. Researchers also compare the differences between fraternal and identical twins. Fraternal twins come from two different fertilized eggs and share only 50 percent of their genes. Identical twins come from a single fertilized egg and share 100 percent of their genes. If the rate of a disease is significantly higher among identical twins than fraternal twins, then researchers conclude genetics are an important factor.

Based on such studies, scientists think there is a strong genetic component to mental health disorders. For example, researchers at the University of Copenhagen in Denmark studied 30,000 pairs of twins in the largest study of schizophrenia in twins to date. Their findings, published in 2017, indicate genetic factors may explain as much as 79 percent of a person's schizophrenia risk. A similarly high estimate of 80 percent has been found for bipolar disorder.

These numbers don't tell a person's actual risk of developing the disease. Rather, they tell the proportion of a person's risk that is explained by genes. Experts call this "heritability." A heritability estimate of 80 percent means that, in most cases of the disease, genetic factors account for about 80 percent of the cause. Nongenetic factors, such as family environment, explain just 20 percent of the cause.

With a 40 percent heritability rate, depression appears to be less heritable than conditions like schizophrenia and bipolar disorder. Yet this still means genes play a very significant role in explaining a person's risk of developing the disorder. For comparison, the heritability of breast cancer is estimated to be roughly 30 percent.

A recent study by a research team from Massachusetts General Hospital may have gone some distance toward identifying a genetic blueprint for depression. The study, which analyzed DNA from more than 300,000 people, pointed to the possible involvement of seventeen specific genetic variations that may be associated with depression in people of European descent.

"Identifying genes that affect risk for a disease is a first step towards understanding the disease biology itself, which gives us targets to aim for in developing new treatments," says Roy Perlis, a coauthor of the study. "More generally, finding genes associated with depression should help make clear that this is a brain disease, which we hope will decrease the stigma still associated with these kinds of illnesses."[26]

Using DNA analysis, researchers are making progress when it comes to other mental disorders too. For example, geneticist Hyun Ji Noh and colleagues at the Broad Institute, a biomedical research center, identified four genes that may be connected to OCD. These genes play an active role in how information is relayed to the prefrontal cortex, the region of the brain where thinking and decision-making take place.

Similarly, a research team of scientists from Harvard Medical School, Boston Children's Hospital, and the Broad Institute found a possible link between schizophrenia and a specific gene involved in a process known as synaptic pruning. This is a natural process in which the brain sheds weak or unnecessary connections between neurons, or brain cells. The researchers hypothesized that people with schizophrenia may have a variant of

> "Identifying genes that affect risk for a disease is a first step towards understanding the disease biology itself, which gives us targets to aim for in developing new treatments."[26]
>
> —Roy Perlis, researcher at Massachusetts General Hospital

Medical researchers look to DNA for clues about the heritability and cause of specific mental illnesses. A disease's heritability rate indicates the proportion of a person's risk for a disease that is related to genes.

the gene that causes the natural pruning process to go wrong. In effect, the gene variation causes excessive synaptic pruning, which makes the brain shed too many neural connections. That disrupts brain circuitry.

This study may also shed light on why schizophrenia tends to emerge in adolescence. According to Beth Stevens, one of the paper's coauthors, the genetic variation may cause "inappropriate pruning during this critical phase of development."[27] During the teen years, most of the brain's synaptic pruning goes on in the prefrontal cortex, the so-called command center of the brain. Overly aggressive pruning in this brain region may lead to the disordered thought processes of schizophrenia.

These findings are promising, but experts caution there are limits to what they can tell us. This is because even when there is a very strong genetic basis for an illness, genes are just one factor in a very complex process. "Genetic factors contribute to almost every human disease by conferring susceptibility or resistance, and, if disease occurs, by influencing severity and progression," neuroscientist Steven Hyman says.[28] Hyman cautions that genes alone don't cause mental illness, though they can make someone predisposed to mental illness. But whether and how those illnesses develop depends on many other interacting factors. These include stressful features in our social environment, exposure to environmental toxins and infections, and even one's own thoughts and psychological states. These factors can trigger a disorder in a person who may already have a genetic risk of developing one.

Environment Matters

As the World Health Organization states, "The capacity for an individual to develop and flourish is deeply influenced by their immediate social surroundings."[29] Research shows exposure to stress and trauma at home or in the broader social environment can have a profoundly damaging effect on teen mental health.

For example, children and teens who are the target of bullying—defined as persistent physical, verbal, emotional, or psychological harassment—are at greater risk than their peers of developing depression. They are also more susceptible to experiencing suicidal thoughts. Similarly, victims of sexual abuse have been shown to have a higher risk of developing depression, anxiety disorders, PTSD, and eating disorders, among other mental health problems.

Other experiences that can negatively impact a teen's mental health include losing a parent, losing another close family member or loved one, growing up in an abusive family environment, experiencing neglect, and living through traumatic events such as natural disasters and acts of violence. Young people who are subject to racism and discrimination may also be especially vulnerable.

Research indicates highly stressful events can produce physical changes in the body and brain. These changes may include the abnormal activity of certain neurotransmitters and elevated levels of stress hormones, such as cortisol. Over time, heightened stress responses can alter how the hippocampus functions. These biological changes can make it harder to manage future stressful situations, which creates a self-perpetuating cycle of dysfunction.

> "The capacity for an individual to develop and flourish is deeply influenced by their immediate social surroundings."[29]
>
> —The World Health Organization

Features in the social environment are not the only factors that can set off profound changes in the body and brain. Aspects of a young person's physical environment can also seriously disrupt the body's ability to function. These influences can start even before birth. For example, exposure to nicotine, alcohol, and other drugs in the womb profoundly affects the fetus's developing brain. In childhood, exposure to toxins such as lead seriously disrupts the chemistry of the brain. All these factors are associated with an increased risk of developing mental health disorders later in life.

There is also evidence that exposure to certain viral and bacterial infections may trigger the development of some mental illnesses. For example, in the 1990s, researchers at the National Institute of Mental

Health discovered some children developed serious cases of OCD after a strep infection (a common infection caused by streptococcal bacteria). Similarly, studies have linked schizophrenia with viral and bacterial infections and with the infectious agent *Toxoplasma gondii*, a parasite sometimes found in cat feces. These pathogens may activate a preexisting susceptibility in a person's genetic makeup.

A Crucial Time

Learning how genes, biology, and environment interact to shape brain function is crucial to understanding why and how mental illnesses develop. It also provides important insight into why adolescence is a peak time for the emergence of such problems.

Childhood and adolescence are stages of life when the brain is especially flexible and responsive to the effects of the environment. Fewer neural patterns have been established, and the architecture of the young brain undergoes rapid growth and change. This means input from the environment can have an especially strong and lasting influence on how a teen's brain develops. These effects on the wiring of the brain will go on to affect future behavior.

In addition, parts of the teen brain that deal with emotions, impulse control, and decision-making are less developed than they are in adults. For example, the prefrontal cortex, which is important for making judgments and regulating emotion, doesn't fully develop until a person's mid-twenties. The onset of puberty also triggers rapid changes in the body's level of hormones, which are the chemical substances the brain produces to regulate growth, sexual development, and other bodily processes. These changes in brain chemistry can affect behavior and mood. As a result, teens may respond differently to stress than adults do. The net effect of these developmental factors is that teens may feel stress more acutely. It may also have a greater effect on the brain.

MIND OVER MATTER

The ability of the brain to "rewire" itself, or to form new patterns of neural connections, is called plasticity. Childhood and early adolescence are periods of peak plasticity. After midadolescence or so, the brain's plasticity declines. New synapses, or connections, are formed less rapidly and there is less flexibility in one's neural architecture. But the plasticity of the brain never disappears altogether. To a certain degree, everything one thinks, sees, and does reshapes the brain and its neural connections.

This means that changing patterns of thinking can literally change the brain's patterns of connections. Jeffrey Schwartz, a researcher at the University of California, Los Angeles, discovered a particularly vivid example of this. He observed that obsessive-compulsive patients who repeatedly resisted a problematic urge and deliberately changed their behavior showed a decrease in brain activity associated with the original problematic urge. He theorized that neurons can become locked into abnormal patterns of activity in patients with a disorder. In effect, the neurons get stuck in a rut. Forcibly changing a behavior pattern forces the neurons, in turn, to change their patterns of firing. This breaks the deadlock. Medications such as Prozac work in a similar way.

Despite the important differences between teen and adult brains, there is a shortage of research specifically on teen mental health. In 2014, less than 1 percent of the National Institutes for Health (NIH) budget went to research on the adolescent brain. And there are relatively few clinical studies focused on understanding how changes in the adolescent brain might affect treatment options. "Too often, children and adolescents are lumped together in large clinical trials with little consideration for how dynamic changes in the brain across development will impact the effectiveness of treatments," says Dr. Francis S. Lee of Weill Cornell Medical College. "This is often compounded by treatments being based on evidence from the adult brain."[30] To better serve the mental health needs of teens, that has to change.

Lifting the Burden of Blame and Shame

All too often, mental health problems inspire blame and shame, as Jill Campbell recounts in her book *A Double-Edged Life: A Memoir of a Young Woman's Journey with Bipolar*. "Although bipolar disorder is a physical condition, I am always aware of the mental illness stigma," she writes. "It is perhaps the most embarrassing and degrading aspect of my disorder."[31]

This stigma is a major reason why so few Americans seek help for mental health problems. According to Dr. John Ratey, recognizing the biological basis of mental illness "can be extremely liberating." He advises, "Simply lifting the burden of blame and shame can be a major first step toward a cure—for the patients, their families, and their care-givers. We don't blame ourselves or feel ashamed when we have a bad back or a physical illness, so why should we impose shame and blame on ourselves when the problem is mental?"[32]

> **"Simply lifting the burden of blame and shame can be a major first step toward a cure—for the patients, their families, and their care-givers."[32]**
>
> —Dr. John Ratey, Harvard Medical School psychiatrist

Chapter 3

WHAT ARE THE EFFECTS OF MENTAL HEALTH PROBLEMS?

Attempts to understand and treat mental illness date back to ancient times. As long ago as the 6000s BCE, Stone-Age humans performed skull surgery to try to release the evil spirits they thought caused mental illness. Ancient Egyptian papyri from 1600 BCE contain references to mental health symptoms such as depression and hysteria. And the ancient Greek physician Hippocrates (470–ca. 377 BCE) classified mental disorders into different types. He prescribed treatments such as drama therapy, or the use of theater and creative expression to promote psychological healing, which is still a recognized form of therapy today.

But although mental health care has a long history, research into child and adolescent mental health is relatively recent. The concept that children and teens can suffer from mental illness did not arise until the end of the nineteenth century. In the United States, serious efforts to treat and prevent mental illnesses in children and adolescents did not begin until the beginning of the twentieth century. Even up until the 1970s, many people thought children and teens were incapable of experiencing certain mental health disorders, such as depression.

As recent research shows, however, depression and other mental health issues are actually quite widespread among young people.

Most people with mental health conditions first started experiencing symptoms when they were teens. According to a National Advisory Mental Health Council report, "Childhood mental health problems and illnesses are common, are on the rise, and impose serious burdens on children and families alike." In fact, the report concluded, "No other illnesses damage so many children so seriously."[33]

Prevalence

Only about 20 percent of teens with a diagnosable mental health disorder get specialized treatment. This makes it hard to come up with precise estimates of how prevalent, or common, mental illnesses are among young people. Because so few people seek help, the actual number of teens with a mental illness is probably much higher than the estimates. In fact, "The number's so large that I think it's hard to wrap our heads around it," says Harold Koplewicz of the Child Mind Institute, a children's mental health advocacy group. "Child and adolescent mental health disorders are the most common illnesses that children will experience under the age of 18."[34]

> **"Child and adolescent mental health disorders are the most common illnesses that children will experience under the age of 18."[34]**
>
> —Harold Koplewicz, the Child Mind Institute

According to the CDC, mental health problems affect at least 15 million American children under the age of seventeen every year. That's roughly one out of five children in the nation. An estimated one out of ten American children and adolescents has a diagnosable mental health disorder severe enough to significantly impact quality of life and the ability to function. The World Health Organization reports similar rates for adolescents ages ten to nineteen years old around the world.

GENDER GAPS

Rates of depression in younger children are the same for girls and boys. Once puberty hits, however, the genders diverge. By midadolescence, girls are more than two times more likely than boys to suffer from depression. According to data from the National Survey of Drug Use and Health, conducted between 2009 and 2014, more than 36 percent of girls reported depression. Just 13.6 percent of boys described themselves as depressed. A similar pattern persists into adulthood.

Experts aren't sure why teen and adult women experience higher rates of depression. Some hypothesize the difference may be linked to sex hormones. This might explain why the rates for girls and boys diverge after puberty. Others speculate that the greater risk for depression in girls may be tied to their vulnerability to gender-based violence, which can cause trauma.

There is also a gender gap between teen girls and boys when it comes to suicide. Teenage girls attempt suicide more than twice as often as teenage boys. However, boys are almost five times more likely to succeed. Experts think the higher success rate for boys may have something to do with differences in the methods used. Girls are more likely to attempt suicide by drug overdose. This comes with a greater chance of being rescued. Boys tend to use more lethal means, such as guns or hanging. Recent evidence, however, shows that rates of suicide by hanging are on the rise among girls.

Anxiety has overtaken depression as the top complaint among college students seeking mental health counseling, according to the Association for University and College Counseling Center Directors. Anxiety is also the most frequently experienced mental health problem among younger teens. In all, more than 6.3 million American teens experience anxiety disorders. That comes to about 30 percent of girls and 20 percent of boys.

An estimated 3 million teenagers between the ages of twelve and seventeen experienced at least one major depressive episode in 2015. More than 2 million of those suffered from depressive symptoms severe enough to disrupt their daily functioning. In total, nearly one-third of young adults in the United States show symptoms of depression, according to the US Department of Health and Human Services.

Double Trouble

Roughly 60 percent of teens with depression also have an anxiety disorder. In general, it is very common for teens to have multiple mental health disorders at the same time. These are called co-occurring disorders. About 40 percent of teens with mental health problems have two or more co-occurring mental health problems. It is also very common for mental health problems to co-occur with an alcohol or drug abuse problem. According to a 2014 National Survey on Drug Use and Health, almost a third of teens ages twelve to seventeen who had a substance abuse problem in 2014 also had a co-occurring mental health disorder. Overuse of alcohol and drugs is particularly harmful to teens because their brains and bodies are still developing at this age.

There seems to be a two-way relationship between mental health problems and substance abuse. Teens struggling with their mental health are more likely to use alcohol or drugs as a way of coping. In turn, substance abuse worsens the symptoms of mental illnesses. For example, because alcohol is a depressant, it can increase feelings of depression and anxiety. Drugs and alcohol can also interact with certain medications, making them less effective at controlling symptoms. And they can impair a person's judgment. This can lead to bad decisions that make the recovery process more difficult. For example, studies have shown that drug abusers are less likely to stick

Teens suffering from mental health disorders are at greater risk of abusing alcohol and drugs. This can lead to a cycle of worsened mental illness symptoms and greater dependency on illicit substances.

with their mental health treatment plan than their counterparts who do not use drugs.

Substance abuse is a major risk factor for suicide. According to the Center for Substance Abuse Treatment, suicide is the leading cause of death among Americans with an alcohol or drug use disorder. Compared to the general population, people treated for alcohol abuse have an estimated tenfold greater risk for suicide. The Center for Substance Abuse Treatment estimates alcohol is a factor in roughly 30 to 40 percent of suicides and suicide attempts. The risk of suicide is even higher among those with a co-occurring mental health problem.

A Growing Problem

Some mental health problems seem to be on the rise among young adults. According to the Department of Health and Human Services, the number of teens experiencing major depressive episodes increased by nearly one-third from 2005 to 2014. In 2015, rates of teen depression were higher than in any other year in the previous decade.

These higher rates of depression have also been accompanied by an uptick in anxiety disorders among young people. In a 2017 survey of health care professionals, 86 percent said they had seen an increase in teen anxiety disorders in the past five years. And according to the American College Health Association, the percentage of undergraduates reporting overwhelming anxiety jumped from 50 percent in 2011 to 62 percent in 2016.

Rates of suicide have also shot up. Hospital admissions for suicidal teens have doubled over the past ten years. Suicides among teenage girls in the United States doubled between 2007 and 2015. For teen boys, the suicide rate rose by more than 30 percent over the same period of time. There has also been a rise in self-harming behaviors in girls. Between 2009 and 2015, the number of ten- to fourteen-year-old girls ending up in the emergency room because of self-inflicted injuries nearly tripled. Among fifteen- to nineteen-year-old girls, incidents of self-harm increased 63 percent during the same time period.

Growing up in difficult socioeconomic circumstances can place stresses on teens. But experts see a rise in anxiety and depression across all demographic groups. According to Arizona State University psychiatry professor Suniya Luthar, there has been a notable rise in anxiety disorders among privileged teens in particular. "There's always one more activity, one more A.P. class, one more thing to do in order to get into a top college," she says. "Kids have a sense that they're not measuring up. The pressure is relentless and getting worse."[35]

Digital Overload

What's behind the rise in anxiety, depression, and other mental health problems? There are undoubtedly many factors at play, but according to some experts, social media, smartphones, and other electronic devices may be a big part of the problem.

Jean Twenge, a professor of psychology at San Diego State University, studies the effects of digital devices on what she calls "iGen"—today's generation of teens, the first to grow up fully in the age of smartphones. Her research shows a link between screen time and psychological distress. The more time teens spend on electronic devices, the more likely they are to report symptoms of depression. Conversely, the less time teens spend looking at screens, the less likely they are to be depressed.

For example, Twenge found that teens who are on their electronic devices for three hours or more a day are 35 percent more likely to have a risk factor for suicide, such as feeling very depressed or thinking about suicide, than teens who engage in less screen time. A study of eighth graders indicated teens who use social media heavily are 27 percent more likely be at risk of depression. "Rates of teen depression and suicide have skyrocketed since 2011. It's not an exaggeration to describe iGen as being on the brink of the worst mental health crisis in decades," she says. "Much of this deterioration can be traced to their phones."[36]

> **"It's not an exaggeration to describe iGen as being on the brink of the worst mental health crisis in decades."[36]**
>
> —Jean Twenge, psychology professor at San Diego State University

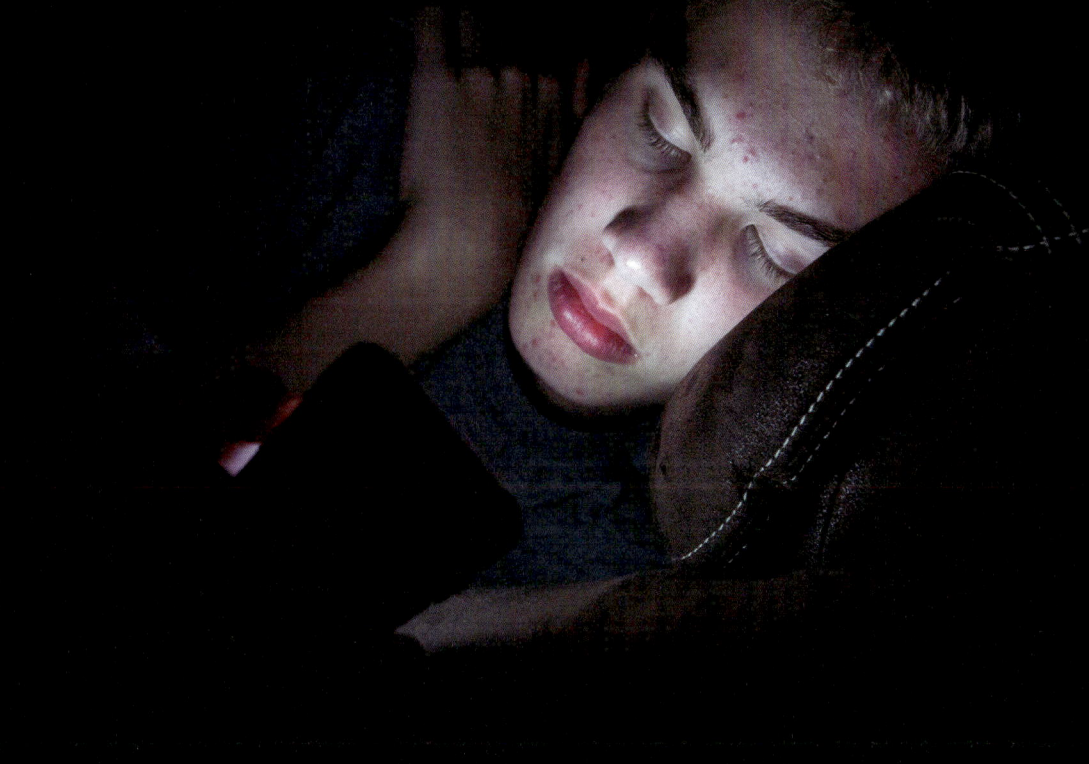

Researchers believe there is a correlation between a rise in teen smartphone usage and an increase in the number of teens suffering from mental health disorders. Many point to social media as the culprit.

    Proving a cause-and-effect relationship between screen time and depression is difficult. However, to many researchers, the link makes sense. Some think social networking sites increase anxiety in teens, who feel the pressure to measure up to impossible standards and unrealistic expectations. This can trigger feelings of inadequacy and low self-esteem. "Kids view social media through the lens of their own lives," says clinical psychologist Jill Emanuele. "If they're struggling to stay on top of things or suffering from low self-esteem, they're more likely to interpret images of peers having fun as confirmation that they're doing badly compared to their friends."[37]

PUTTING DOWN THE PHONE

When her sixteen-year-old daughter, Nina, attempted suicide, Christine Langdon was taken completely by surprise. "Nina was funny, athletic, smart, personable," she says in a *Time* magazine feature on teens and smartphone use. "[D]epression was just not on my radar."[1] Nina's therapist identified body image insecurity as the root of her depression. Nina pinned much of the blame on social media:

"I was spending a lot of time stalking models on Instagram, and I worried a lot about how I looked," Nina says, describing how she would stay up late, glued to her smartphone. Low self-esteem, lack of sleep, and the stress of an eating disorder made her depression spiral out of control.[2]

The Royal Society for Public Health in the United Kingdom warns that sites like Instagram can promote a "compare and despair" attitude in teens. Viewing staged and heavily edited photos may make teens feel bad about themselves. Jean Twenge's advice to teens like Nina is to "put down the phone, turn off the laptop, and do something—anything—that does not involve a screen."[3]

1. Quoted in Markham Heid, "We Need to Talk About Kids and Smartphones." *Time*, October 10, 2017. www.time.com

2. Quoted in Heid, "We Need to Talk About Kids and Smartphones."

3. Jean M. Twenge, "Have Smartphones Destroyed a Generation?" *The Atlantic*, September 2017. www.theatlantic.com

Others worry too much screen time means less time for other activities that are important for healthy human lives, such as in-person socializing. Research shows socializing enhances our sense of well-being, while isolation can worsen depression. "Human beings are social animals," says Brian Primack, director of the University of Pittsburgh's Center for Research on Media, Technology, and Health.

"We evolved over millions of years to respond to eye contact and touch and shared laughter and real things right in front of us."[38] Yet teens are spending less and less time hanging out face-to-face with their friends. The number of teens who regularly get together with their friends fell by more than 40 percent between 2000 and 2015. And only about 56 percent of high school seniors went on dates in 2015, compared to 85 percent in earlier generations.

An Urgent Need

Whether or not smartphones or social media are to blame, the trend is clear: more and more teens are struggling with anxiety, depression, and other mental health issues. But while teen mental health problems continue to become more prevalent, the availability of services has not kept up with the demand. The American Academy of Child and Adolescent Psychiatry (AACAP) warns there is a critical shortage of trained professionals specializing in the mental health needs of children and teens. As of 2016, only an estimated 8,500 psychiatrists across the nation specialized in the care of children and adolescents. This is far below the roughly 30,000 that the AACAP estimates are needed. The shortage is especially great in rural and high-poverty areas.

According to psychiatrist Michael Brody, "Children who need specialized psychiatric care are suffering because of the lack of child and adolescent psychiatrists."[39] Many receive no care at all. Many of those who do receive care end up relying on services offered through schools and child welfare agencies. All too often, these services are poorly coordinated. Treatment is often subpar. According to the National Advisory Mental Health Council, "The majority of treatments and services children and adolescents receive in the community have either not been evaluated to determine their effectiveness or are simply ineffective."[40]

The result is that far too many mental health disorders among young people go undiagnosed and untreated. These disorders tend to persist into adulthood, often worsening. And the longer the lag time between the onset of a mental health problem and the start of treatment, the harder—and more costly—the problem is to treat.

The Personal Price of Mental Illness

Adolescence is a crucial formative period of life. How well teens do in school can determine their future academic opportunities, career paths, and earning potential. The habits and skills teens develop shape how well-adjusted and stable they will be as adults. Their interpersonal interactions and experiences set the tone for how well they will be able to navigate society in the future. Failing to treat teen mental health problems can disrupt these important developmental years. The repercussions can extend long into adulthood.

Having an untreated mental illness as a teenager is associated with a slew of adverse outcomes, including a higher rate of teen pregnancy, greater risk of substance abuse, and lower level of educational achievement. Teens with mental disorders are more likely to fail a grade or be suspended from school. And the high school dropout rate for teens with mental health problems is higher than that of any other disability group. Roughly 50 percent of teens with a mental illness drop out of high school.

> **"Children who need specialized psychiatric care are suffering because of the lack of child and adolescent psychiatrists."[39]**
>
> —Michael Brody, psychiatrist

Failure in school imposes lifelong costs on teens. High school dropouts have a higher unemployment rate, are more likely to live in

TREATMENT RECEIVED BY ADOLESCENTS WITH MAJOR DEPRESSIVE EPISODES

Despite the long-term consequences of untreated mental health disorders, only 40 percent of adolescents suffering from a major depressive episode received any kind of medical care between 2015 and 2016.

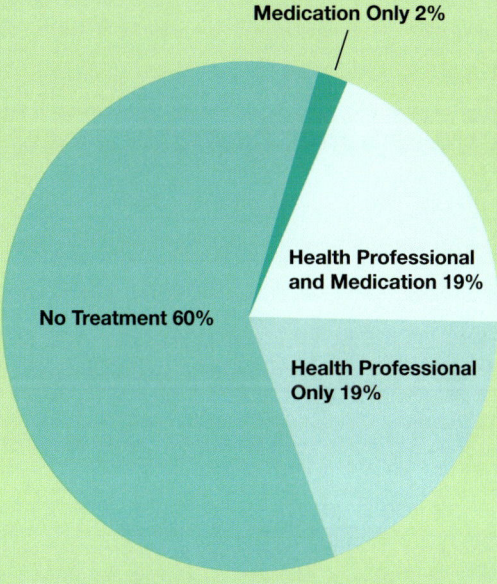

"Statistics," *National Institute of Mental Health*, January 2018. www.nimh.nih.gov.

poverty, and earn significantly less than their counterparts with a high school diploma or higher. According to US Census Bureau data, the average high school dropout earned an income of $20,241 in 2012. That's 34 percent less than the average high school graduate income of $30,627 and 64 percent less than the typical college graduate income of $56,665.

High school dropouts also face a greater risk of ending up in jail. According to the Child Mind Institute, 68 percent of inmates in state prisons have not finished high school. And just over 70 percent of youth caught up in the juvenile justice system meet the criteria for a diagnosable mental health disorder. When young people with mental health problems end up in jail instead of receiving appropriate treatment, they pay an enormous personal price in lost potential. Being convicted of a crime affects a person's future employment prospects, disrupts personal goals and family life, and all too often perpetuates a cycle of underachievement and social marginalization.

Social Costs and Consequences

Teen mental health problems that persist untreated into adulthood can have lasting effects on a person's quality of life. But the costs are not just personal. Mental illness also imposes steep costs on society. "Mental health costs are the highest single source of global economic burden in the world," says Francis Lee, professor of psychiatry at Cornell Medical College."[41]

This burden includes the cost of care—an estimated $147 billion in the United States in 2009 alone. It also includes indirect costs, such as lost income from unemployment, expenses for social services and disability support, and the cost of incarceration. Former National Institute of Mental Health director Thomas Insel estimates the total economic burden of mental disorders in the United States reached at least $467 billion in 2012. To put that figure into context, that is more than the direct and indirect financial costs of diabetes, respiratory disorders, and cancer put together.

These costs rise exponentially when mental health disorders start early in life. Untreated, early onset disorders tend to worsen over time. This means they become more costly to treat. Teens with mental health problems are more likely to drop out of school,

The teenage years are a particularly vulnerable time, especially for those dealing with mental illness. Early diagnosis and treatment helps prevent negative outcomes and costs later in life.

end up in jail, or become unemployed later in life, which causes an increase in the indirect economic burden on society. According to Lee, "Mental illnesses that emerge before adulthood have a tenfold higher cost than those that emerge later in life."[42] Thus, improving access to high-quality mental health care is not just critical for millions of American teens—it is also important for the social and economic health of the nation. As the National Advisory Mental Health Council says, "Our ability to create a promising future for the country depends, in part, on our ability to ensure that all children have the opportunity to meet their full potential and live healthy, productive lives."[43]

Chapter 4

HOW CAN TEENS GET HELP?

Without treatment, mental illnesses take a heavy toll on individuals, families, and society. Untreated mental health problems can disrupt family life, derail personal growth and achievement, and cost society billions of dollars. Yet with treatment, most people with a mental illness get better. According to the National Alliance on Mental Illness (NAMI), between 70 and 90 percent of affected individuals show significant improvement with appropriate treatment. With early identification and treatment, the success rate is even higher.

Tricky Business

Recognizing the signs of mental health problems can be tricky. Symptoms can vary from person to person. Not everyone experiences all the same symptoms. And not everyone experiences the same symptoms the same way. Identifying warning signs can be particularly hard in teens. Some teens exhibit their depression through irritability and aggressiveness, which parents and teachers may mistake as signs of ordinary behavior problems. Other symptoms may be dismissed as typical teenage angst. As adolescent mental health experts Terje Ogden and Kristine Amlund Hagen write, "For both anxious and depressed youth, knowing where to draw the line

It can be difficult to discern between normal teenage feelings and those associated with mental illnesses such as anxiety or depression. Trained and licensed professionals can help with that.

between what is normal adolescent worry and gloomy demeanor on the one side and pathological anxious and depressed symptomology on the other is difficult."[44]

That's why many experts recommend routine mental health screening in schools and doctor's offices. "Mental health screenings—whether in school or out—should be as routine as any other health screenings, such as those for eyesight or hearing," mental health practitioner Kita Curry says. "They would not only ensure kids don't fall behind because of a delay in treatment, but also would help erase

> "Mental health screenings—whether in school or out—should be as routine as any other health screenings, such as those for eyesight or hearing."[45]
>
> —Kita Curry, mental health practitioner

the stigma of mental illness that stops people in need from reaching out."[45]

Routine mental health screenings facilitate the early identification of mental health problems. They can make teachers, parents, and teens themselves more aware of early warning signs. And they can help connect teens who may be at risk with resources for help. However, screenings do not take the place of consultation and evaluation with a specialist. And they are not intended to be a diagnostic tool. As James Mazza, a University of Washington psychologist, says, "Screening doesn't do diagnosing. It's just a measure to say, 'How are things going on in your life?' Then a counselor can follow up and do a risk assessment interview or make an appropriate referral to someone who can do the risk assessment."[46]

Where to Start

Many teens receive mental health services through their schools. These services may be offered by school counselors, school psychologists, or school social workers. But there are also many other sources of help and information available for teens experiencing mental health issues.

National organizations such as NAMI are rich sources of information on mental illnesses, including practical advice on seeking treatment and links to other organizations. There are also many specialized national organizations focusing on specific problems, such as the Anxiety Disorders Association of America and the Depression and Bipolar Support Alliance. These and other organizations offer many of their resources online.

Other sources of help include support groups and national hotlines. Support groups are peer-led groups that offer a safe community for sharing experiences and gaining insight and advice from others who are experiencing similar challenges. Hotlines provide immediate help in an emergency situation. For example, the National Suicide Prevention Lifeline is a twenty-four-hour toll-free crisis hotline. It connects callers with their local crisis center, putting them in touch with immediate help in their area. NAMI also operates a toll-free hotline during regular business hours, connecting callers with trained volunteers who can provide mental health information, support, and even referrals. The nonprofit Mental Health America provides contact information for these and other hotlines, as well as mental health information. Its national website includes a searchable directory of local affiliates, including support groups and resources in specific areas.

Finding a Provider

A family doctor or pediatrician is usually not a specialist in mental health issues, but they can give referrals to professionals who are. Another trusted adult, such as a school counselor or member of the clergy, may also be able to find specialized help. Many national organizations offer searchable directories of mental health care providers, including the American Academy of Child and Adolescent Psychiatry, the American Medical Association, and the American Psychological Association. Local offices of national organizations such as Mental Health America are another good source of information about local programs and services.

A parent or guardian's insurance company can provide a list of participating providers. Those who have insurance will want to

#LETSTALK

According to the 2015 Montana Youth Risk Behavior Survey, almost one-third of the state's teens said they felt sad and hopeless almost every day for at least two weeks in a row. After reading such statistics, high school sophomores Keely Drummond and Maggie Andrews paired up with Nicole Zimmerman, program coordinator for the Alliance for Youth, a nonprofit organization in Great Falls, Montana, to help design and promote an app to raise awareness about depression. "I don't think a lot of people know what it is and how drastically it affects some people's lives," Andrews says.[1]

Called #LetsTalk, the app allows users to create a profile and track warning signs for depression in themselves and their friends. Through the app, users can also find contact numbers for support, including the National Suicide Prevention Line, and locate a designated safe place where they can find an adult to talk to for support. "It's a great tool at your fingertips," Zimmerman says. "We all have our phones. The app has a lot of good information that I hope [teens] never need, but if they do, it's there."[2]

1. Quoted in Sarah Dettmer, "Belt Students Say #LetsTalk with New App for Teen Mental Health," *Great Falls Tribune*, November 30, 2017. www.greatfallstribune.com

2. Quoted in Dettmer, "Belt Students Say #LetsTalk with New App for Teen Mental Health."

be sure to locate health care providers who accept their insurance plan. For those without insurance, there are a range of low-cost options. State Medicaid offices can provide a list of practitioners who accept Medicaid.

Community health centers also offer low-cost health services. These are state-funded centers offering services prioritized for low-income families. The federally operated Healthcare.gov site provides a searchable database of community health centers. And the Substance Abuse and Mental Health Services Administration's Health

Information Network (SHIN) has a Mental Health Facilities Locator that can connect teens with local treatment facilities, including affordable mental health services. Contact information about community health centers can also be found online or at a public library.

Unfortunately, new patients may have to wait a long time before they are able to get an appointment. "Access to specialty mental health care is limited," says psychologist Dr. Clare Purvis. "In most settings, wait times for an appointment are prohibitively long."[47] In these cases, NAMI recommends asking to join a provider's waiting list for cancellations. That way, if another patient cancels at the last minute, there may be an unexpected opening for an appointment. Most importantly, if there is an urgent problem, people should seek other sources of help in the meantime. "If you feel you can't wait weeks or months for help, see your primary care doctor as soon as possible to get treatments and support to tide you over until you have your team assembled," the NAMI website says. "And if you're in an emergency situation, please go immediately to a hospital emergency room."[48]

Who to See

Mental health providers are professionals trained to diagnose mental health problems and provide appropriate treatment. There are many different kinds of providers, however, and it can be hard to know who is the right one to consult.

Psychiatrists are trained and licensed medical doctors who specialize in diagnosing and treating mental and emotional illnesses. Like all doctors, psychiatrists have earned a medical degree, gone through years of training, and are licensed to prescribe medication.

Unlike psychiatrists, psychologists are not medical doctors and so are not licensed to prescribe medication. However, they are trained to diagnose mental health problems and to provide various types of therapy and counseling, including individual and group therapy. They may work as a team with a psychiatrist or other doctor who can prescribe medication if needed. Psychologists have a PhD degree in psychology and at least two years of supervised professional training.

There are several other types of mental health professionals who also specialize in therapy and counseling. The most common types are mental health counselors and clinical social workers. These practitioners typically have master's degrees and cannot prescribe medication. Mental health counselors are trained to provide one-on-one therapy and counseling to help people work through their emotions, develop coping strategies, and tackle a specific set of problems related to a mental health disorder. Social workers also provide therapy and counsel patients in need in addition to a wider range of social services. For example, a social worker may help patients find resources they can use in their communities, work with the school system to solve a problem, or help with housing or financial issues that may be a source of anxiety or stress.

> **"If you feel you can't wait weeks or months for help, see your primary care doctor as soon as possible to get treatments and support to tide you over until you have your team assembled."[48]**
>
> —National Alliance on Mental Illness

Which type of provider is the best choice will depend on the patient's specific needs. "Good mental health professionals . . . should have some knowledge of the full range of treatment options, as well as expertise in treating disorders that fall into areas covered by their practice," clinical psychologists David J. Bridgett and Michelle M. Lilly write.[49]

In many cases, patients may end up working with more than one mental health provider, such as a psychiatrist to manage medications, a psychologist or other health care provider for therapy, and a social worker to help manage their case and connect them with other support services. Whatever choice patients make, they need to make sure their providers are licensed to practice in their state. Teens and their guardians will also want to make sure they pick professionals who are trained to work with young people and have expertise in their specific mental health problems.

Getting Diagnosed

Diagnosing a mental health disorder can be a long process. The first step is to rule out other medical conditions. In some cases, physical illnesses can cause symptoms similar to those of a mental illness. Thyroid conditions, for example, can create symptoms of depression. Hypoglycemia, or low blood sugar, can sometimes cause feelings of delirium, a disturbed state of mind characterized by delusions and incoherence. Symptoms such as depression can also be a side effect of certain medications. Whatever the cause, these symptoms need medical attention. However, they are not considered features of a mental health disorder unless other medical conditions have been ruled out. That is why the process of diagnosing mental health problems typically starts with a physical exam.

Unlike for physical illnesses, there are no lab tests for mental illnesses. Instead, most mental health diagnoses in the United States are made based on the *DSM*. Published by the American Psychiatric Association, the *DSM* aims to be an exhaustive catalog of recognized mental disorders. It classifies a wide range of disorders into categories and lists defining symptoms for each. Mental health care providers use the *DSM* to evaluate whether a patient's symptoms meet established criteria for specific diagnoses. Insurance companies use it to decide whether patients should be reimbursed for treatments.

Before making a diagnosis, mental health providers conduct a thorough psychological evaluation. This includes interviewing patients about their symptoms, thoughts, behavioral patterns, and feelings. The health care provider may also interview parents and teachers or perform behavioral observations. Patients may fill out questionnaires or take cognitive tests that assess intelligence and personality.

"Frankly, going through all this testing can be a pain," Cait Irwin says about her own diagnosis process. "I got tired of people poking around inside my mind. It serves a useful purpose, though, because it helps your treatment providers understand your problems and identify likely causes. Armed with this information, they can design a treatment plan that's custom-tailored to your individual needs."[50]

Treatment Options

Because everyone is different, a treatment that works for one person may not work for another. That's why patients and their care providers have to work together closely to determine what kind of treatment plan will work best. Which specific type of treatment and how much of it a person needs will vary depending on the illness and the severity of the symptoms. Other factors also play a role. These include individual personality, coping skills, and a person's family and social environment. The two main treatment options for most mental health disorders are medication and psychotherapy, also known as talk therapy. Many patients receive a combination of both types.

Medication targets the underlying biology of an illness while therapy uses psychological methods to help patients work through emotional, social, and behavioral challenges. Trained therapists help patients talk through and explore their feelings, experiences, and

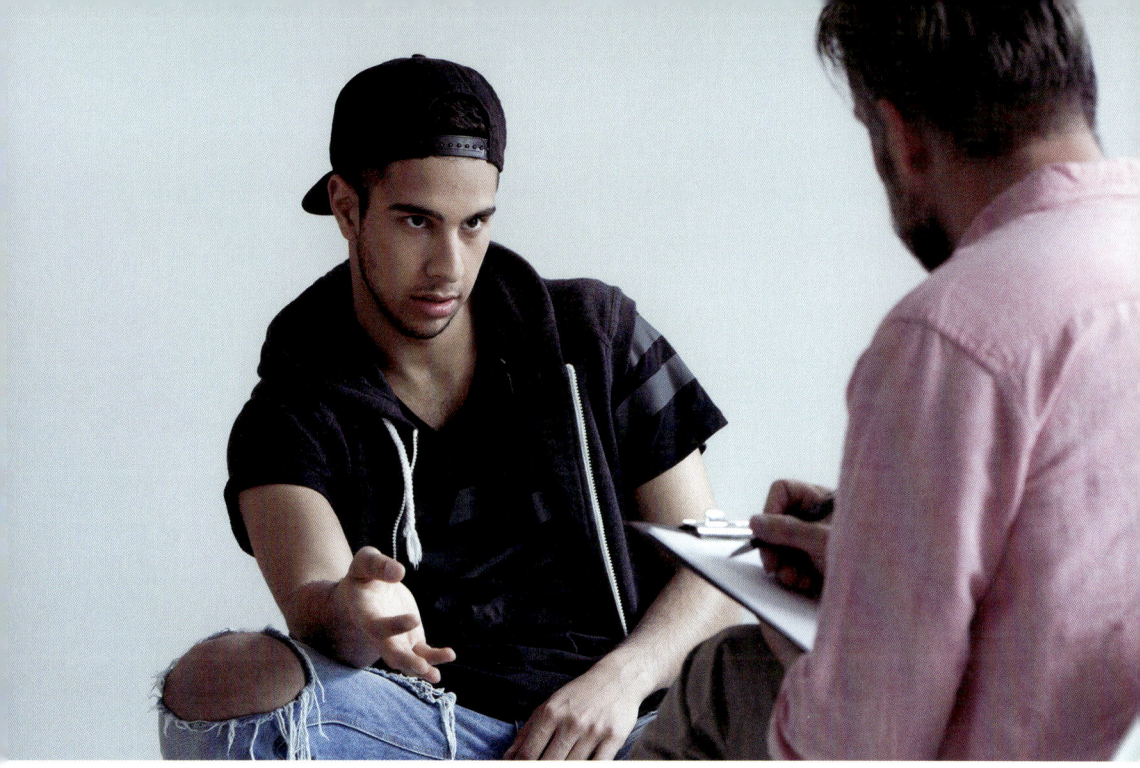

Treatment for mental illnesses begins with a thorough evaluation of the patient's behaviors and emotions. It may also involve a physical examination to rule out any other illnesses.

problems. The aim is to help patients develop greater self-awareness and understanding, develop techniques for managing their problems, and replace harmful habits of thought and behavior with more constructive ones. In the process, therapy may also reshape the brain circuitry that underlies problematic behaviors and thoughts.

Psychotherapy

Psychotherapy is most commonly used for depression, anxiety, and panic disorders. It can also be used to treat other conditions, including eating disorders, PTSD, bipolar disorder, OCD, substance use disorder, and self-harming behaviors.

Psychotherapy can be done individually or in group and family settings. There are also many different varieties and approaches. One of the most common is cognitive behavioral therapy (CBT), which aims to help patients change problematic patterns of behavior and cognition, or thinking. The idea behind CBT is that one's perceptions and attitudes affect how one feels emotionally. Thus, if a person can develop new attitudes toward objects of anxiety or new ways of thinking about her problems, then she will feel more emotionally healthy. In CBT, the therapist helps the patient to identify negative patterns of thoughts and self-defeating behaviors and replace them with more positive ones.

In some cases, this involves what experts call exposure therapy. This is a process of gradually exposing a person to something they fear so that, over time, they become more desensitized to it. This reduces the fear and anxiety response. For example, a person with severe social anxiety may be gradually exposed to carefully controlled situations where they are forced to confront their social phobias. The goal is for the patient to understand these situations are not dangerous. The process works by gradually rearranging the circuits of the brain. Eventually, being in those situations will no longer set off the neural connections in the brain that create feelings of fear and anxiety.

CBT is the most well-researched form of psychotherapy for treating teen depression and anxiety. Clinical studies confirm its effectiveness. A 2008 study published in the *New England Journal of Medicine* showed that young adults had a higher improvement rate using CBT (60 percent) than the antidepressant medication Zoloft (55 percent). The most effective treatment, however, was a combination of the two treatments. More than 80 percent of those studied improved when they received both medication and CBT.

Medication

Zoloft is a type of medication known as a selective serotonin reuptake inhibitor (SSRI). SSRIs work by regulating the level of serotonin in the brain, a neurotransmitter thought to play a key role in depression

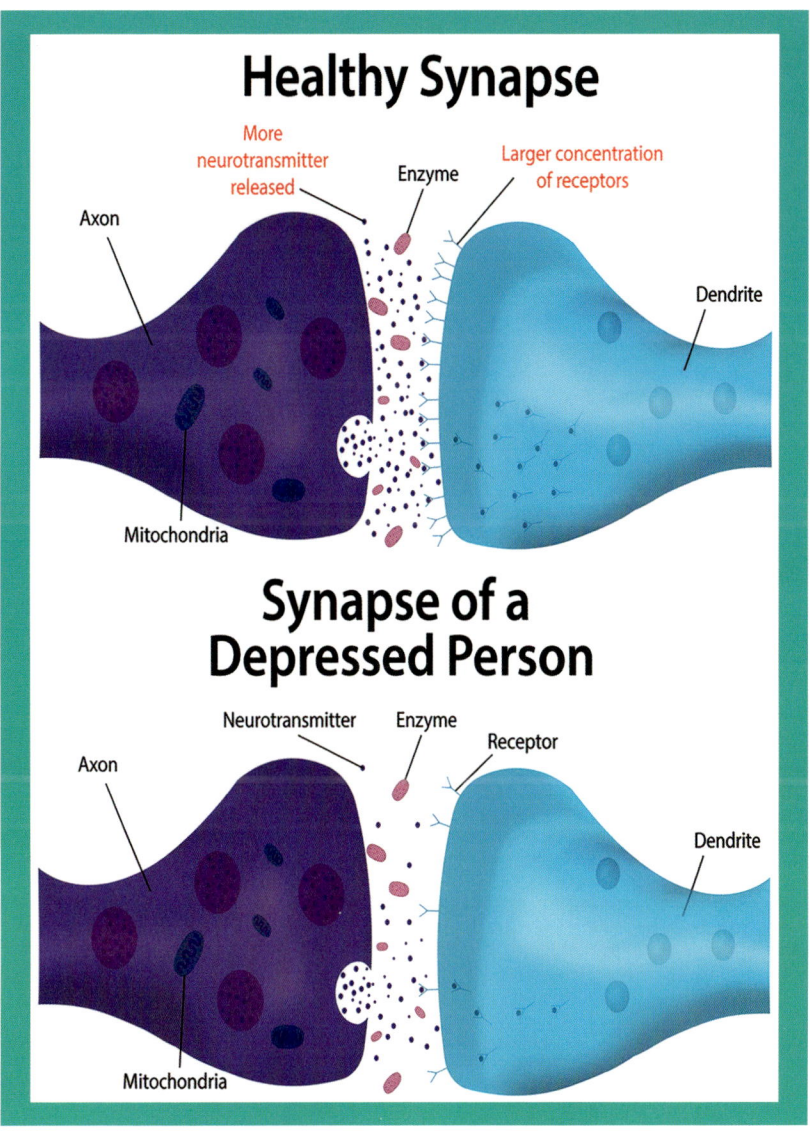

Depression is often linked to a lack of the neurotransmitter serotonin. SSRIs boost the amount of serotonin between synapses, which can relieve the symptoms of depression.

and anxiety. Developed in the 1990s, SSRIs are the antidepressants most commonly prescribed for teens. There are other classes of antidepressants that work differently, such as selective norepinephrine reuptake inhibitors (SNRIs), which block the reabsorption of serotonin and norepinephrine, but as of 2017 only SSRIs had been approved by the US Food and Drug Administration (FDA) for use in children and teenagers.

In addition to treating depression and anxiety disorders, SSRIs can also be used to treat other mental health issues, including OCD. For teens, they are the most commonly prescribed medications. But many other types of medication exist as well, including mood stabilizers, which are used to control the violent mood swings of bipolar disorder. Antipsychotics are used to manage the symptoms of psychosis and schizophrenia.

Experts caution that particular care must be taken when prescribing medication for children and teens. There has been much less research on the safety and effectiveness of mental health medications on young people. Medications that may be safe and reliable for adults may affect the developing brain differently.

All medications, whether prescribed for teens or adults, can cause side effects. Common side effects of medications prescribed for mental illnesses include excessive tiredness, headaches, heartburn, restlessness, and weight gain or loss. Many side effects are mild, and some prove to be temporary, disappearing after the body has time to adjust. However, medications can sometimes lead to permanent and severe side effects. All use of medication should be closely monitored by a qualified psychiatrist, who can adjust doses and prescriptions as needed. Each person's brain is different, so there is no one-size-fits-all prescription. What works for one person may not work for another.

Treatment Settings

Many mental health issues are primarily treated on an outpatient basis. This means that patients are not required to stay overnight at a treatment center. Instead, they visit a clinic or health provider's

ALTERNATIVE MENTAL HEALTH CARE

A growing number of people are turning to alternative medicine to improve their mental health. "Alternative medicine" describes health and wellness remedies that are not part of conventional Western medicine. This includes mind–body healing techniques such as meditation and hypnosis, a technique in which clinicians help individuals reach a state of heightened mental relaxation and focus. Derived from traditional Chinese medicine, acupuncture is another popular alternative therapy. Acupuncturists insert special needles at specific sites of the body that are thought to promote both physical and mental healing.

Herbal supplements and vitamins are also touted as alternative mental health remedies. Some people believe that St. John's Wort, which is derived from a flowering plant, is useful in easing the symptoms of depression. Omega-3 essential fatty acids may be helpful for mood stabilization. These are a group of chemicals naturally found in certain foods, including fish. The vitamin folate, also called folic acid or vitamin B9, may enhance the effectiveness of conventional antidepressants.

Alternative mental health therapies may have a role to play in a person's treatment plan. But experts warn that many of these methods have not been well studied. Unlike prescription medications, herbal supplements are not reviewed by the FDA. This means there is not substantial, unbiased evidence of their effectiveness or safety. Some alternative therapies and over-the-counter medicines may also have negative interactions with prescription medication. That's why it is imperative to consult with a doctor before taking new medications or supplements.

office for treatment sessions on specific days of the week or month. Occasionally treatment may require a hospital stay. Typically this is when a person poses a danger to others or there is a high risk of serious self-harm. In Cait Irwin's case, for example, hospitalization became necessary when she developed persistent suicidal thoughts.

"Ultimately," she says, "the hospital gave me a safe place to catch my breath and regain my footing."[51] In most cases, hospitalization lasts about three to five days, or until the patient has stabilized. During the stay, the patient receives specialized care and is monitored twenty-four hours a day. The hospital setting offers a safe, controlled place where patients can work past the crisis point and resolve the risk of harm.

There are times when patients need to stay in an overnight facility for longer periods. This may happen when a patient needs intensive treatment over several months for symptoms that do not get better on an outpatient basis. In these cases, treatment often occurs at a residential treatment facility, which is a live-in facility that provides medical care in a more comfortable setting than an inpatient hospital. Depending on a person's particular needs, residential programs incorporate a range of treatments, including medication and various types of therapy, along with other support services. In the case of eating disorders, for example, treatment for teens "typically includes individual and group therapy, creative therapy (such as art, music, and writing), academic services, nutrition classes, and recreational activities," says Carrie Arnold, who chronicles her struggle with anorexia in her memoir *Next to Nothing: A Firsthand Account of One Teenager's Experience with an Eating Disorder*. "Most people stay in a residential program for several months, which I have found to be necessary to break the cycle of the eating disorder," she writes.[52]

Finding the Wellness in Illness

Seeking professional treatment is essential to the recovery process for teens with mental health problems. In addition to getting professional treatment, however, there are also important changes teens can make in their everyday lives. Many of them are simple and ordinary, such as eating nutritiously, exercising, and getting enough sleep.

"Critics sometimes claim that a focus on 'ordinary' measures like exercise and diet is too simplistic to affect ordinary behavior," Dr. John Ratey says. "Not so."[53] In fact, more than one thousand studies have documented that exercise can affect mental health. For example, a randomized controlled trial conducted by researchers from Duke University Medical Center showed that depressed adults who exercised improved as much as those treated with the antidepressant Zoloft. Research by Jasper Smits of the Anxiety Research and Treatment Program at Southern Methodist University shows that exercise can have similar benefits when it comes to anxiety disorders. In a 2008 study, participants in a two-week exercise program showed significant improvement in their anxiety symptoms compared with a control group.

> "Critics sometimes claim that a focus on 'ordinary' measures like exercise and diet is too simplistic to affect ordinary behavior. Not so."[53]
>
> —Dr. John Ratey, Harvard Medical School psychiatrist

Like exercise, sleep may also play an important role in mental health. Psychologist Jean Twenge wonders whether sleep deprivation could be a factor linking heavy smartphone use to increased rates of depression and anxiety. Studies have shown that teens who spend more time online are more likely to sleep less. Studies have also shown that lack of sleep is correlated with a variety of mental health problems, including depression and anxiety. For example, a 2017 study of more than 3,700 British college students showed that treating sleep problems also reduced levels of anxiety and depression. "Having insomnia doubles your chances of developing depression and we now know that if you treat the insomnia it reduces depression," says Daniel Freeman, a coauthor of the study from the University of Oxford. "If you can sort out your sleep, you could also be taking a significant step forward in tackling a wide range of psychological and emotional problems."[54]

By themselves, eating well, sleeping more, and exercising are not cures for mental illness. But they can play an important role in increasing a person's overall health and well-being. This can foster greater resilience and make it easier to cope with challenges. Finding a fulfilling hobby or vocation can also be a lifeline. This can provide an important source of personal meaning and value. For Irwin, fostering her love of art played a crucial role in her recovery. "I looked for activities that fed my soul and threw myself into them with profound intensity," she writes in her memoir. "Taking part in a productive hobby is a hopeful, positive act that serves as a powerful antidote to depression."[55]

Elyn Saks echoes this point. Saks is a distinguished law professor at the University of Southern California. In 2009, she was awarded a MacArthur Foundation Fellowship, also known as a "genius grant," a prestigious award bestowed on people who show exceptional talent in their field. Yet as a young college student, she was diagnosed with schizophrenia and told that she would never be able to live independently or hold down a job.

How was Saks able to beat the odds? Therapy and medication were a critical element of her treatment. However, Saks also credits another essential ingredient in her success: her work. Despite receiving such a bleak prognosis from her doctors, Saks continued her studies and immersed herself in her work. This gave her focus, purpose, and fulfillment. In turn, this sense of purpose and value anchored her in her struggles. Saks calls this "finding the wellness within the illness." Along with therapy and medication, she says, this should be a therapeutic goal of treatment. "Doctors should urge their patients to develop relationships and engage in meaningful work," she writes. "They should encourage patients to find their own

Treatment of and recovery from mental health disorders requires a certain amount of self-care. Added to a healthy lifestyle, artistic, athletic, musical, and intellectual hobbies can be a major source of relief.

repertory of techniques to manage their symptoms and aim for a quality of life as they define it. And they should provide patients with the resources—therapy, medication and support—to make these things happen."[56]

RECOGNIZING SIGNS OF TROUBLE

Every mental health disorder has its own symptoms, but there are certain common signs of trouble that can indicate a possible mental health issue. One or two on their own are not cause for alarm, but experiencing several at once may indicate the need to consult with a mental health professional. Those with suicidal thoughts or thoughts of harming others need immediate attention.

Teens may need help if they:

- Feel confused, on edge, angry, upset, worried, or scared most of the time
- Feel intense sadness or feelings of hopelessness and dread that last for at least two weeks at a time
- Experience frequent stomachaches or headaches with no obvious physical explanation
- Have trouble concentrating, thinking clearly, or making decisions
- Lose interest in things they used to enjoy
- Start avoiding friends, family, and social activities
- Have trouble keeping up in school, or grades decline
- Experience unexplained changes in sleeping or eating habits
- Frequently feel exhausted, with little or no energy
- Have an excessive fear of gaining weight
- Experience severe mood swings
- Have persistent thoughts and memories that feel out of control
- Hear voices or see things that are not there
- Deliberately harm themselves
- Abuse alcohol or drugs
- Have thoughts of suicide

ORGANIZATIONS TO CONTACT

American Foundation for Suicide Prevention
afsp.org

AFSP is an organization that provides research, education, and advocacy to the fight against suicide.

Anxiety and Depression Association of America
adaa.org

ADAA is a nonprofit organization dedicated to the prevention, treatment, and cure of anxiety- and depression-related disorders.

Depression and Bipolar Support Alliance
www.dbsalliance.org

DBSA is a group that works to help improve the lives of people who have mood disorders.

Mental Health America
www.mentalhealthamerica.net

MHA works to address the needs of those living with mental illness and to promote the overall mental health of all Americans.

National Institute of Mental Health
www.nimh.nih.gov

NIMH works to transform the understanding and treatment of mental illnesses through basic and clinical research, paving the way for prevention, recovery, and cure.

SOURCE NOTES

Introduction: Erasing the Stigma of Mental Illness

1. Cait Irwin, Dwight L. Evans, and Linda Wasmer Andrews, *Monochrome Days: A Firsthand Account of One Teenager's Experience with Depression.* New York: Oxford University Press, 2007, pp. 6–7.

2. National Institute of Mental Health, *Teen Depression Study: Understanding Depression in Teenagers*, 2016. www.nimh.nih.gov.

3. Irwin, Evans, and Andrews, *Monochrome Days: A Firsthand Account of One Teenager's Experience with Depression*, p. ix.

4. Irwin, Evans, and Andrews, *Monochrome Days: A Firsthand Account of One Teenager's Experience with Depression*, p. xiv.

5. David Satcher, "Mental Health: A Report of the Surgeon General–Executive Summary," *Professional Psychology: Research and Practice*, February 2000. www.psychosocial.com.

6. Irwin, Evans, and Andrews, *Monochrome Days: A Firsthand Account of One Teenager's Experience with Depression*, p. ix.

Chapter 1: What Is Mental Health?

7. American Psychological Association, *Change Your Mind About Health*, n.d. www.apa.org.

8. World Health Organization, *Fact Sheet: Mental Health: Strengthening Our Response,* April 2016. www.who.int.

9. U.S. Department of Health and Human Services, Substance Abuse and Mental Health Services Administration, Center for Mental Health Services, National Institutes of Health, and National Institute of Mental Health, *Mental Health: A Report of the Surgeon General*, 1999. nlm.nih.gov.

10. Terje Ogden and Kristine Amlund Hagen, *Adolescent Mental Health: Prevention and Intervention.* Abingdon, UK: Routledge, 2013, p. 72.

11. Linda Wilmshurst, *Essentials of Child Psychopathology.* Hoboken, NJ: John Wiley & Sons, 2005, p. 104.

12. John J. Ratey, *A User's Guide to the Brain: Perception, Attention, and the Four Theatres of the Brain.* New York: Vintage, 2001, p. 232.

13. Andrea Petersen, *On Edge: A Journey Through Anxiety.* New York: Crown, 2017, p. 5.

14. Anushka Pai, Alina M. Suris, and Carol S. North, "Posttraumatic Stress Disorder in the DSM-5: Controversy, Change, and Conceptual Considerations," *Behavioral Sciences*, 7.1, 2017.

15. Wilmshurst, *Essentials of Child Psychopathology*, p. 230.

16. Wilmshurst, *Essentials of Child Psychopathology*, p. 230.

17. Patrick E. Jamieson, *Mind Race: A Firsthand Account of One Teenager's Experience with Bipolar Disorder*. New York: Oxford University Press, 2006, pp. 2, 4.

18. Jamieson, *Mind Race: A Firsthand Account of One Teenager's Experience with Bipolar Disorder*, p. 4.

19. Brian Gabriel, "The Evolutionary Advantage of Depression," *Atlantic Monthly*, October 2, 2012. www.theatlantic.com.

20. Gerald Koocher and Annette La Greca, *The Parents' Guide to Psychological First Aid: Helping Children and Adolescents Cope with Predictable Life Crises*. New York: Oxford University Press, 2011, p. 325.

21. Victoria Leatham, *Bloodletting: A True Story of Secrets, Self-Harm and Survival*. Oakland, CA: New Harbinger Publications, 2006, pp. 2, 5.

Chapter 2: What Causes Mental Health Problems?

22. Eric R. Kandel, "A New Intellectual Framework for Psychiatry," *American Journal of Psychiatry*, 155.4, 1998, p. 460.

23. Vilayanur S. Ramachandran, *The Tell-Tale Brain: A Neuroscientist's Quest for what Makes Us Human*. New York: WW Norton & Company, 2012, p. 14.

24. Lisa Rapaport, "People with Anxiety May Be Hard-Wired to See World Differently," *Reuters,* March 7, 2016. www.reuters.com.

25. Jim Dryden, "Low Serotonin-Receptor Levels Linked to Depression," *The Source*, January 1, 2002. source.wustl.edu.

26. Massachusetts General Hospital, *Novel Study Method Identifies 15 Genomic Regions Associated with Depression*, August 1, 2016. www.massgeneral.org.

27. Benedict Carey, "Scientists Move Closer to Understanding Schizophrenia's Cause," *New York Times*, January 27, 2016. www.nytimes.com.

28. Steven E. Hyman, "The Genetics of Mental Illness: Implications for Practice," *Bulletin of the World Health Organization*, 78, 2000, pp. 456, 457.

29. World 29 Organization, *Risks to Mental Health: An Overview of Vulnerabilities and Risk Factors*, 2012. www.who.int.

30. Francis S. Lee et al, "Adolescent Mental Health—Opportunity and Obligation," *Science*, 346.6209, 2014, pp. 547–549.

SOURCE NOTES CONTINUED

31. Jill Campbell, *A Double-Edged Life: A Memoir of a Young Woman's Journey with Bipolar*. Bloomington, IN: AuthorHouse, 2009.

32. Ratey, *A User's Guide to the Brain: Perception, Attention, and the Four Theatres of the Brain*, p. 357.

Chapter 3: What Are the Effects of Mental Health Problems?

33. National Advisory Mental Health Council Workgroup on Child and Adolescent Mental Health Intervention Development and Deployment, *Blueprint for Change: Research on Child and Adolescent Mental Health*, 2001. www.nimh.nih.gov.

34. Kate Snow and Cynthia McFadden, "Generation at Risk: America's Youngest Facing Mental Health Crisis," *Today*, December 12, 2017. www.today.com.

35. Benoit Denizet-Lewis, "Why Are More American Teenagers Than Ever Suffering From Severe Anxiety?" *New York Times*, October 11, 2017. www.nytimes.com.

36. Jean M. Twenge, "Have Smartphones Destroyed a Generation?" *The Atlantic*, September 2017. www.theatlantic.com.

37. Rae Jacobson, "Social Media and Self-Doubt," *Child Mind Institute*, n.d. childmind.org.

38. Markham Heid, "We Need to Talk About Kids and Smartphones," *Time*, October 10, 2017. www.time.com.

39. American Academy of Child and Adolescent Psychiatry, *Child and Adolescent Workforce Crisis: Solutions to Improve Early Intervention and Access to Care*, n.d. www.aacap.org.

40. National Advisory Mental Health Council Workgroup on Child and Adolescent Mental Health Intervention Development and Deployment, *Blueprint for Change: Research on Child and Adolescent Mental Health*.

41. Lee et al, "Adolescent Mental Health—Opportunity and Obligation."

42. Lee et al, "Adolescent Mental Health—Opportunity and Obligation."

43. National Advisory Mental Health Council Workgroup on Child and Adolescent Mental Health Intervention Development and Deployment, *Blueprint for Change: Research on Child and Adolescent Mental Health*.

Chapter 4: How Can Teens Get Help?

44. Ogden and Hagen, *Adolescent Mental Health: Prevention and Intervention*, p. 77.

45. David Heitz, "Should Schools Screen Kids for Mental Health Problems?" *Healthline*, August 29, 2015. www.healthline.com.

46. Brendan Borrell, "Pros and Cons of Screening Teens for Depression," *LA Times,* September 16, 2014. www.latimes.com.

47. Nicole Spector, "Why Don't Americans Get Regular Mental Health Checkups? It's Complicated," *NBC News*, January 22, 2018. www.nbcnews.com.

48. National Alliance on Mental Illness, *Finding a Mental Health Professional*, n.d. www.nami.org.

49. David J. Bridgett and Michelle M. Lilly, "What Type of Mental Health Professional Is Right for You?" *Psychology Today,* May 30, 2013. www.psychologytoday.com.

50. Irwin, Evans, and Andrews, *Monochrome Days: A Firsthand Account of One Teenager's Experience with Depression*, p. 67.

51. Irwin, Evans, and Andrews, Monochrome Days: A Firsthand Account of One Teenager's Experience with Depression, p. 64.

52. Carrie Arnold. *Next to Nothing: A Firsthand Account of One Teenager's Experience with an Eating Disorder.* New York: Oxford University Press, 2007.

53. Ratey, *A User's Guide to the Brain: Perception, Attention, and the Four Theatres of the Brain*, p. 357.

54. Nicola Davis, "Lack of Sleep Could Contribute to Mental Health Problems, Researchers Reveal," *The Guardian*, September 6, 2017. www.theguardian.com.

55. Irwin, Evans, and Andrews, *Monochrome Days: A Firsthand Account of One Teenager's Experience with Depression*, pp. 104, 109.

56. Elyn R. Saks, "Successful and Schizophrenic." *The New York Times*, January 27, 2013. www.nytimes.com.

FOR FURTHER RESEARCH

BOOKS

Lisa Bakewell, ed., *Mental Health Information for Teens*. Detroit, MI: Omnigraphics, 2014.

Dale Carlson and Dr. Michael Bower, *Out of Order: Young Adult Manual of Mental Illness and Recovery*. Branford, CT: Bick Publishing, 2013.

Lorena Huddle and Jay Schleifer, *Teen Suicide*. New York: Rosen Publishing, 2012.

Andrea Petersen, *On Edge: A Journey Through Anxiety*. New York: Crown, 2017.

Jennifer Shannon, *The Anxiety Survival Guide for Teens: CBT Skills to Overcome Fear, Worry, and Panic*. Oakland, CA: Instant Help Books, 2015.

Jacqueline B. Toner and Claire A. B. Freeland, *Depression: A Teen's Guide to Survive and Thrive*. Washington, DC: Magination Press, 2016.

Christopher Willard and Mitch R. Abblett, *Mindfulness for Teen Depression: A Workbook for Improving Your Mood*. Oakland, CA: New Harbinger Publications, 2016.

INTERNET SOURCES

Child Mind Institute. *2016 Children's Mental Health Report*. n.d. www.childmind.org.

Benoit Denizet-Lewis. "Why Are More American Teenagers Than Ever Suffering From Severe Anxiety?" *The New York Times*, October 11, 2017. www.nytimes.com.

Susanna Schrobsdorff. "Teen Depression and Anxiety: Why the Kids Are Not Alright." *Time*. October 27, 2016. www.time.com.

Jean M. Twenge. "Have Smartphones Destroyed a Generation?" *The Atlantic*, September 2017. www.theatlantic.com.

WEBSITES

The Jason Foundation
www.jasonfoundation.com

The Jason Foundation provides information and educational resources to raise awareness about teen suicide and work for its prevention.

OK2TALK: Help for Youth
www.ok2talk.org

OK2TALK aims to create a safe online community where young people struggling with mental health challenges can openly talk about their experiences without fear of stigma. Users are encouraged to share their personal stories, messages, poems, photos, videos, and other posts.

TeenMentalHealth.org
www.teenmentalhealth.org

A nonprofit educational organization, TeenMentalHealth.org develops training programs, publications, tools, and resources for improving mental health care for teens and young people.

INDEX

agoraphobia, 13–14
alcohol, 15, 16, 32, 39–40
alternative medicine, 63
American College Health
    Association, 41
American Psychological Association,
    8, 53
Anderson, Michael, 25
antidepressants, 60–63, 65
anxiety, 10–13, 15, 20, 24–26, 31,
        38–39, 41–43, 45, 52, 59–63, 65
    biological function of, 12
    and the brain, 24
    and stress, 12
    support for, 52
    treatment of, 59–60, 62–63, 65
    triggers, 13, 42–43
Arnold, Carrie, 64

bipolar disorder, 17–18, 28, 35,
    53, 62
brain, 22–27, 29–34
    development, 33–34
    imaging techniques, 24, 26–27
    and mental health disorders,
        24–26, 29–32
    structural changes, 25–26, 32
Brody, Michael, 45

Campbell, Jill, 35
Center for Substance Abuse
    Treatment, 40

Centers for Disease Control and
    Prevention, 19, 37
cognitive behavioral therapy
    (CBT), 60
computer tomography (CT), 24
co-occurring disorders, 39
Curry, Kita, 51

depression, 5, 12, 15–20, 25–29, 31,
        36, 38–39, 41–42, 44–45, 47,
        53–54, 57, 59–60, 62, 65–66
    biological functions of, 19
    and gender, 38
    and genes, 28–29
    and the immune system, 19
    support for, 53
    and technology, 42–44
    treatment of, 47, 59–60, 62, 65–66
*Diagnostic and Statistical Manual of
    Mental Disorders* (*DSM*), 11, 15, 57

eating disorders, 11, 59, 64
exercise, 65
exposure therapy, 60

fear, 12–15, 60
fight or flight, 12
Food and Drug Administration, US,
    62, 63

GABA, 25
generalized anxiety disorder, 13
genes, 27–33

Hagen, Kristine Amlund, 10, 50
health services, 53–55

hippocampus, 25, 26, 32
Hyman, Steven, 31

iGen, 42–45
Irwin, Cait, 4, 6–7, 58, 63–64

Jamieson, Patrick, 18
Jason Foundation, 20

Koocher, Gerald, 20
Koplewicz, Harold, 37

La Greca, Annette, 20
Langdon, Christine, 44
Leatham, Victoria, 21
Lee, Francis, 48
#LetsTalk, 54
Luthar, Suniya, 41–42

major depressive disorder, 16, 19
mania, 17–18
Mazza, James, 52
medical insurance, 53–54, 57
medication, 58, 60–64, 66
mental health, 8–10, 27–31, 45,
    51–53, 55–56, 65
  counselors, 56
  and exercise, 65
  and genes, 27–31
  hotlines, 53
  providers, 45, 53, 55–56
  screening, 51–52
  and sleep, 65
mental illness, 5–11, 22–27, 29,
    31–33, 35–37, 46–50, 53, 57–58
  and the brain, 22–27
  consequences and costs, 46–50
  diagnosis, 57–58
  and environmental factors, 32–33
  and genes, 31
  signs of, 9
  stigma of, 5–7, 10, 29, 35, 51–52
  symptoms of, 11
  treatment of, 37–40, 45–46, 48,
    50, 54–55, 58–66
mood disorder, 16, 26

National Alliance on Mental Illness
    (NAMI), 50, 52, 53, 55
neurons, 22–25, 29, 34, 60
neurotransmitters, 22–23, 26, 32, 61
Noh, Hyun Ji, 29
non-suicidal self-injury (NSSI),
    20–21, 59

obsessive-compulsive disorder, 11,
    29, 33–34
Ogden, Terje, 10–11, 50

panic attacks, 13–14
Paz, Rony, 25
Perlis, Roy, 29
persistent depressive disorder, 16
Petersen, Andrea, 13–14
post-traumatic stress disorder
    (PTSD), 14–15, 25, 31, 59
psychiatrists, 55, 57
psychologists, 55–57
puberty, 4–5, 9, 33

Raison, Charles, 19
Ratey, John, 12, 35, 65

Saks, Elyn, 66–67
Satcher, David, 5–6
schizophrenia, 11, 22, 25, 27–31, 33,
    62, 66
Schwartz, Jeffrey, 34
self-harm, 20–21, 59
serotonin, 26, 60
sexual abuse, 15, 31
sleep, 5, 16, 18, 44, 64–66
social anxiety disorder, 13
social media, 42–45
social workers, 56–57
Stevens, Beth, 30
stigma, 5–7, 10, 29, 35, 51–52
stress, 8, 10, 12, 14, 19, 24–27,
    31–34, 41, 44, 56

INDEX CONTINUED

substance abuse, 15–16, 39–40, 59
suicide, 19–20, 31, 38, 40–42, 44, 53
support groups, 53
synaptic pruning, 29–30

terminology, 17
therapy, 58–59, 64, 66
trauma, 14–15, 31–32
Twenge, Jean, 42–44, 65
twins, 27–28

Wilmshurst, Linda, 11, 15
World Health Organization, 19, 31, 37

X-rays, 24

IMAGE CREDITS

Cover: © fizkes/Shutterstock Images

7 (top left): © Albert H. Teich/Shutterstock Images

7 (top right): © Tinseltown/Shutterstock Images

7 (middle left): © JStone/Shutterstock Images

7 (bottom): © Petr Toman/Shutterstock Images

7 (middle right): © Kathy Hutchins/Shutterstock Images

9: © pathdoc/Shutterstock Images

14: © tlorna/Shutterstock Images

18: © Jacob Lund/Shutterstock Images

21: © Martin Novac/Shutterstock Images

23: © MriMan/Shutterstock Images

30: © Gorodenkoff/Shutterstock Images

40: © Stokkete/Shutterstock Images

43: © mooremedia/Shutterstock Images

49: © Monkey Business Images/Shutterstock Images

51: © Monkey Business Images/Shutterstock Images

59: © Photographee.eu/Shutterstock Images

61: © joshya/Shutterstock Images

67: © Jacob Lund/Shutterstock Images

ABOUT THE AUTHOR

Elisabeth Herschbach is an editor and writer from Washington, DC.